An Uncertain Pilgrim

All That Life Has to Offer
A Spiritual Wisdom Guide for You

(c) 1997 J Patrick Ware, MD All Rights Reserved
ISBN: 09658224-4-3 $19.95 U.S. Softcover

By J Patrick Ware, MD

Presented by: AWare Publishing, POB 871149, Stone Mountain, GA 30087
Phone: 404-561-2526 Fax: 770-806-0658 E-mail: DRJIMPAT@aol.com
Web Site: anuncertainpilgrim.com

Reviews by: NAPRA (Holiday, 1997), Small Press Magazine: (11/97), &
Metaphysical Reviews (8/97) Available through: My Therapist's Bookstore: 888-
292-9356; Ingram Book Co: 800-830-7915; Bookpeople: 800-999-4650;
New Leaf Dist Co: 770-948-7845; All Border's stores: 800-644-7733;
ProMotion Publishing Co: 800-231-1776; & Amazon.com

Come take the journey of a life time, experience and live the Rainbow!

An Uncertain Pilgrim

ALL THAT LIFE HAS TO OFFER

A SPIRITUAL WISDOM GUIDE FOR YOU

J. Patrick Ware, MD

AN UNCERTAIN PILGRIM
All That Life Has To Offer, A Spiritual Wisdom Guide For You

Copyright © 1997 J. Patrick Ware, M.D.   *C-1*
P.O. Box 15429, Atlanta, Georgia 30333

Cover Artwork and Illustrations: Margaret Estes
Cover and Book Design: Webster Design
Copy Editing: Kathryn A. Langner and Virginia Gurley

Library of Congress Cataloging-in-Publication Data
Ware M.D., J. Patrick
An Uncertain Pilgrim:
All That Life Has To Offer, A Spiritual Wisdom Guide For You
by J. Patrick Ware, M.D.

ISBN 0-9658224-4-3

Dedication

To all those who have sought, are seeking and will seek to understand the very essence of our gift of life

To my parents for their gifts of life and undying challenge, inspiration, and affection

To my sister for her enduring loyalty, support and devotion

To my children for their unwavering love and respect

To Kathryn for her steadfast, enduring support and faith

To all those who have traveled, loved, and shared their life time with me

Acknowledgments

As this book has emerged from the depths of all of me, I am aware that those who have contributed to the book are those people who have in any way contributed to my life. The origins and sources of my learning have been many and diverse and the numbers of people who have been willing to offer their gifts of knowledge and experience in varied manner are legion. It is impossible to adequately individually enumerate and honor each. It is with profound reverence and gratitude that I honor all of my teachers and their gifts.

For her passion for truth and inspiration and her diligent, tireless effort in support of this book, I am deeply grateful to Kathryn Langner.

For my family, thank you for your love, integrity, industry and faith.

For my friends, I am ever aware of your fraternity, sense of adventure and encouragement.

For my teachers, I am grateful for your creativity, service, commitment and excellence.

For my colleagues, I respectfully acknowledge your leadership, teachings and challenges to our profession.

For my fellow Pilgrims, I am continuously appreciative of your courage, inspiration and trust.

TABLE OF CONTENTS

CHAPTER ONE 13
   Am I A Pilgrim?
   Is This Just Another Goodie Goodie Book?

CHAPTER TWO 33
   Beginning The Journey

CHAPTER THREE 43
   Who Are You? Who Am I?
   Let Us Be Properly Introduced

CHAPTER FOUR 53
   On Becoming Aware
   Learning About Learning

CHAPTER FIVE 71
   Understanding Attachment

CHAPTER SIX 87
   Understanding Loss

CHAPTER SEVEN 97
   The Nature of Fear

CHAPTER EIGHT 107
   Beginning to Know and Understand One's Self

CHAPTER NINE 129
   Focus, Self Vs Distraction
   Discipline & Patience

CHAPTER TEN 139
   Experience the Universal Basis of Truth
   Practicing To Be & Living the Adventure

CHAPTER ELEVEN 147
   The Journey
   Experience the Relief, Freedom, and Creativity

CHAPTER TWELVE 167
   Opportunities for Pilgrims as Teachers
   Solicitation of Your Stories of Discovery

CHAPTER THIRTEEN 173
   The Continuation of Your Learning
   The Pilgrim's Journey

EXERCISES 183
   Taking The Journey

ADDENDUM 215
   Supportive Resources
   Relevant Additional Factors

I never suspected that I would have
to learn how to live - that there were
specific disciplines and ways of
seeing the world I had to master
before I could awaken to a simple
happy, uncomplicated life.

- Dan Millman

CHAPTER ONE

Am I
A Pilgrim?

Is This
Just Another
Goodie Goodie Book?

He who is outside the door has already a
good part of his journey behind him.

- Dutch Proverb

What if someone told you that contentment and creativity were readily accessible, cheap, if not out right free, and much simpler and perhaps even easier than your present reality? Would you like to exchange your Inner Turmoil and Conflict for Peace and Tranquility? Are you interested in a Complete and True Appreciation of All That Life Has to Offer?

With a gentle tap on your shoulder, let me speak to you of possibilities, and perhaps even hold your heart ever so gently. Life is a journey and as we travel we pass TIME, step by step and day by day. The Journey is the Commonality of the SEARCH for MEANING and THE DESIRE TO IMPROVE THE QUALITY OF LIFE! What percentage of people you know are genuinely pleased with their lives and experience contentment and creativity as integral parts of their moment-to-moment journey? How many people do you believe would be interested in enhancing their ability to access these experiences?

Much wisdom is available from those who have gone before us as we search for Truth and Meaning. I have been graced by the company and trust of many Pilgrims and have learned much from each and every one. You have many wonderful "secrets" within and you may uncover them. All humans seek freedom...freedom to be—to express—to know. It is an experience of vulnerability and courage, a discovery from within. It is living all of life as all of who you are.

Walk with me, if you will, and those who have gone before you. With humility and grace let us begin the exploration of the human spirit.

After years of involvement with myself and other fellow travelers, only some of whom are "patients", many have suggested the sharing of the information contained herein in a format which will allow other Pilgrims access to these experiences who might otherwise not be able to avail themselves. The challenge: to create a simple learning resource in written form—A PERSONAL GUIDE. The idea: to facilitate the learning, understanding, and preservation of one of nature's most splendid and endangered species—the human spirit itself!

Who is this Personal Guide for? Not for those who are resistant to considering something new or different! It is for those who seek their truth—an open heart—and to know themselves fully. It is for those who are willing to face the chaos within and experience pure creativity, pure knowledge, and pure spirit. Humankind has avoided their truth for centuries because of fear of pain and loss. WHAT IF? the chaos is simply a negotiable threshold that has kept us away from incredible experiences and beauty that lie within? A Challenge: WHAT IF? there is something to all of this? Who loses if there is value and substance to these realities and you don't PURSUE, READ, PONDER, EXPLORE, LEARN,

*

What if?

the Chaos

is simply

a negotiable

threshold

*

CREATE, AND TEACH WITH PATIENCE AND DELIBERA-
TION?! Who wins?

The reader now has a dilemma!

Is this about an alternative way of living, experiencing life
and availing one's self of life's opportunities? Would you turn
down a potentially life enhancing experience without fully
exploring it? How many times have you turned down a new
experience only to realize later, sometimes even years later,
the original decision was very regrettable? How many times
have you seen others take the immediate "easy" way avoiding something new with the clear conviction that the avoidance was actually the long term "easy" way? As an observer,
you knew that they were making their life MORE difficult,
not less, yet you were unable to effectively convey the wisdom of your observations.

How many times have you inwardly known you were
doing the Same Thing and told yourself **with *great* internal
effort** whatever INTERNAL DECEPTIONS you would buy at
the time to allow yourself to continue without change? How
many times have you wondered, "Is there another way?"
"Have I misplaced my trust in relationships? or 'stuff' or
'power'?" Have these resources actually paid the dividends
you seek? For whatever reasons—**you have persisted with a
"system" you are not pleased with.**

You may be quietly lonely, struggling with feeling empty,
inadequate, dependent, out of control, vulnerable, afraid
and dissatisfied. The overall success of your life may be dis-
appointing regardless of your many tangible achievements.
Do you think that personal happiness and contentment are
achievable options only for others because they have abilities you do not or because there is "something wrong" with
you that prevents such an achievement? You may indeed be

unable to fully imagine individual personal independence that is natural, spontaneous, and genuinely creative.

I regret not getting to know you personally. A direct exchange would clearly be more desirable. However, you will find that the simplicity and availability of this format accomplishes the same result of making this an effective, personal, live learning experience. If you pursue and persist, you will be able to understand the importance of and ability to maintain your awareness of self—YOUR SELF FOCUS. You will understand the relationship of self-awareness to mood, self-esteem, impulses, self-respect, energy, motivation, feelings, concentration, intimacy, freedom, aloneness vs loneliness, solidarity vs emptiness, and creativity! You will understand that the dreaded feelings of "needing" to be connected or attached to something or someone are NOT bad but are very natural and essential survival drives which can be satisfied COMPLETELY!

I will from time to time emerge out of the text as a live Pilgrim. I'll be there all through your journey and there are many other individual, human resources available to assist you as well. (Please refer to the Addendum, page 215.) You will, if you CHOOSE, join the DISCOVERY community and experience an awakening of your spirit. You may eventually realize that you have abilities of which you were unaware. You may also enjoy the awareness that most of what we will be exploring you already knew or suspected! Your initial self-deprecatory experience will evolve into a sense of radiance and joy. Congratulations on your new beginning! Celebrate yourself as a new student and as a teacher of other Pilgrims in your own right!

Discovery Is Learning

How can you explore the ideas and experiences offered in this Guide in such a way as to optimize the opportunity presented? Are there different ways of getting this information and experience into your inventory of assets? In fact, there are many variables relevant to the learning of this material. **The most important is that your journey be an experience rather than an intellectual endeavor.**

As we learn any new set of ideas and experiences, our success is based on our accessibility, motivation, focus, perseverance, exploration, and trial and error. This opportunity is no different. How often do we assume that adequate self awareness is either unnecessary or will come with minimal or no effort? The significance of "distraction" in the pursuit of any goal is enormous and as we will see, the harbinger of the loss of the self. How often do our expectations lead to disappointments? We will learn how these disappointments become distractions to our learning about ourselves. When the attention of the student is focused away from the subject at hand, this distraction impedes the natural acceptance of new information. The primary goal of full and complete learning about self is halted when an individual focuses on anticipated achievement rather than on current and ongoing experiences. When we focus on **who we want to be** rather than **who we are**, that expectation becomes the foundation for our distraction and disappointment.

Learning happens most quickly when the barriers to learning are removed. One does NOT **MAKE** learning happen. The early lessons of medicine teach that the sickest kidney is smarter than any physician. The physician's first role is to "do no harm." One does not **MAKE** a sick kidney healthy. Often, the natural process is not only better but, believe it or not EASIER!

How can you begin a journey that you do not understand? Can you imagine thinking in Japanese or Russian? Do people in "despair" have anything in common? How would you describe the quality and nature of your own personal awareness? Have you ever felt helpless or hopeless? Have you ever ignored a haunting inner sense of any of these unpleasant experiences? WHAT IF? the "sickness" or "something wrong" with you that you continue telling yourself is an insurmountable barrier is actually an absence of understanding of how to change? Wouldn't that make at least some Pilgrims actually students? Is ignorance an illness in need of a diagnosis or a student in need of a teacher?

The most honest position of a new Pilgrim is to acknowledge the uncertainty concerning the unknown—Herself! Welcome to the New World of your DISCOVERY—a world that challenges the differences between "I can't", "I haven't", and "I won't!" I can't because it's too hard. I haven't because I don't know how. I won't because I'm afraid to change. How hard is the easy way? WHAT IF? you do know how and simply need listen to the whisper within? Change is the only constant. Regardless of how we may attempt to keep things the same, they are always changing either by withering away or blossoming to new growth. You may discover that a barrier to your joy has been your unwillingness to change.

WHAT IF? Discovery is simply Learning—a primary process and paradigm—essential to understand before approaching ANY new subject? Learning has many common elements, as well as individually specific components, and not all "would be" students readily understand how they best learn. Because the ability to learn is such an individu-

ally specific process and because it is a function of accessibility, there are "good" teachers and "not so good" teachers.
Students have long recognized that merely understanding a
subject does not a teacher define. How bright does a newborn have to be to become fluent in her native language,
and how quickly does she learn?

You may discover many potential barriers to your enlightenment which, in the moment, are experienced as forbid-
ding or even dangerous to approach. People readily confuse
the current inability to do or perform a new task as the
inability to learn. Fear of failure or adversity often fuels a
position of "I won't." This refusal to proceed produces the
expected lack of success and pain of anticipated inadequacy.
The problem, of course, is that these barriers prevent forward movement and discovery. Advanced age is even given
by some as one inherent barrier to the acquisition of understanding and learning. Yet, our Native People teach us that
learning and wisdom are indeed strongholds of the aged.
WHAT IF? the laws that govern learning are the same for you
as for that newborn? WHAT IF? the only real difference may
have been that you were more resistant to learning? **There is
really no rank among Pilgrims.** Those Pilgrims who tap their
hidden resources will find life's tasks more approachable,
inviting and achievable.

How many times do genuinely bright people take a look
at something completely foreign to them and exclaim, "I
could never do that!" We "feel" we can't and then accept that
feeling as the end of the issue. "Wouldn't it be 'nice' if I
could do something like that?!" WHAT IF? the much feared
learning experience is actually **the last real frontier—your
own mind and ability?** WHAT IF? **that which you have**
avoided—yourself and your full ability to know and achieve—

is the greatest untapped resource in existence? WHAT IF? your basic ability is thoroughly unknown to you and waiting for your discovery?

What do you have if you don't have self respect? Can you even imagine having self-respect? WHAT IF? you don't know what self-respect actually is and you don't even know that? WHAT IF? you do not have self-respect and are unaware of this? Innumerable Pilgrims predictably exclaim after being "in therapy" (beginning their journey of "self study") something to the effect of: "I had no idea I was depressed...until I began looking... I only had a sense that something wasn't O.K. or just wasn't right!" It is often easier to understand our life situations retrospectively, when the emotional charge is less negative or painful, such as the true value of the experience of poverty becoming more clear and intense **after** the acquisition of assets.

Can you imagine experiencing most difficult tasks including the pain life brings to you as opportunities for personal growth rather than insurmountable tasks? One would then convert barriers into opportunities, oppression into expression and shackles into freedom. The remembered initial fear of riding a bike becomes a genuine source of pleasure and expression. The task presented herein is the opportunity to learn about one's self which may shift the fear and avoidance of not knowing to an opportunity for pleasure and expression in discovery.

A Simple Truth: Man and Woman made in God's or a Higher Power's image find the greatest answers to life's questions from the most intimate source and relationship life has to offer—THE SELF. Some are merely delayed in the timing of their appreciation of the incredible simplicity of the workings of the human spirit and the secrets of the human mind. We are all on a progressed path, each of us evolving in response to our free will choices. Some of us choose now to awaken to the spirit within and others of us will choose to continue exploring life in repetitious patterns of self avoidance and denial, at least, for now.

Would one consider taking a solitary trip across the desert on a camel one knew nothing about? I would venture that most would try to avoid the trip, ignore the camel (hoping you had been "given" a good one) or extend minimal energy in the direction of finding out the camel's strengths, weaknesses, and unrealized potential. Or, one might put effort into enhancing the camel's abilities prior to the trip. Do you really want to avoid your life's trip? **Do you really want to simply hope that you will be "given" adequate resources to truly get the most from your JOURNEY? Should you simply accept that your maximum ability to live is defined only by what you have been able to achieve to date?** What is the problem with just continuing on with the way you and possibly everyone in your family has done it for generations? **Who loses** if you don't explore alternatives to your current way of approaching yourself and your life? **If you don't learn about alternatives, you will not have choices.** Perhaps, you know all too well what your current method of approaching life is bringing you, although you may not fully understand how and why you are making your current choices.

This manual offers an opportunity to develop at least one ALTERNATE choice concerning the way you live your life. It does NOT seek to "make" anyone different. Once fully explored and integrated, this new manner of living may be easily retired in favor of your old, if you so desire. I have, by the way, not run into anyone who, after fully exploring the nature and essence of this alternative manner of approaching life's opportunities, has chosen to resume his former choices. There are, however, many students who, as they go along the learning path, periodically put down the learning and resume "the old ways." This is an **essential** part of learning anything new. You will not trust the success of the new way until you have put it to the test and more than likely returned to your old way so that you may once again "reevaluate" just how bad the old way really was! The memory of success is short, and I am confident that if you are genuinely interested in exploring new options, and if you persevere with supportive personal and/or professional assistance as needed, you will "**Get There.**"

Using This Guide

The actual textbook is yourself, NOT this manual. This manual is offered as a blueprint or guide to the individual. It is intended to stimulate interest, to challenge, and to inspire motivation, as well as to make available these relatively simple and effective approaches to those who may otherwise never know of them. Please carefully consider the intellectual vs the experiential dimensions of approach to this material. The profound differences between What we Think and How we Feel are the differences we naturally recognize that exist between the world of thought and that of the Human Spirit itself. Humankind unsuccessfully continues to attempt to govern the world of feelings and the spirit with intellect. The spiritual realm exists within as a foundational element, and you may find it is the simplest expression of the presence of life itself. The spiritual does not in any respect respond to intellectual constraint or government by ideas. Ideas cannot manage the spirit.

You, yourself, must experience the process and content of this book—not simply read the text. If you choose to merely approach the experience offered intellectually, you will follow an old, familiar and unsuccessful path. You must "do" this book to take the journey and allow yourself a new beginning. Access to your spiritual presence awaits within and is Not discoverable with ideas alone.

With 25 years experience in Medicine/Psychiatry (listening) and 50 years as a person (living) with a background in labor, learning, love, loss, formal religion, athletics, business, the professions, education, politics, hobbies, success, failure, parenthood, sex, sickness, death, birth, poverty and affluence, I am pleased and honored to share my experiences with you. These life experiences are for all Pilgrims primary instructional sources in and of themselves, as well as sources for learning about learning. You will find that as you teach others, you will experience a continuation of your learning and one of the most rewarding aspects of your journey.

As I have pursued my own personal journey, I am reminded of my first recollections of awareness which go back to poignant feelings at the age of two of a fearful incident in which I was injured. The feelings are clear in my mind although the specific events are blurred. I remember precisely the fear and instinctive desire to seek the assistance of my father because I knew he would know what to do. I found myself, I am told, with a deep cut to my head with much bleeding. The experience in the moment was one of extreme fear, uncertainty, and overwhelming vulnerability. Upon the arrival of my father at the scene, I was comforted. It is clear to me now that my primary concern at that time had more to do with the attachment to my father than the actual physical needs of the moment. Security and well-being were indeed defined by attachment since I became calm with the appearance of my father before any injury assessment or treatment could be offered. Therein lies the beginning of my journey. My earliest recollection of feelings define for me the beginning of awareness. As you begin your journey, your early recollections will poignantly accompany your current reflections. The actual birth of the human spirit begins with the first awareness. These past experiences of awareness are the foundations of your spiritual enlightenment and await your rediscovery.

There are barriers to learning about the self which we choose to avoid crossing. These include the avoidance of pain, self-doubt and dishonesty, and the fear of the unknown and/or failure. A primary barrier to full spiritual awareness is the **avoidance of emotional pain.** This elusive discovery is an integral aspect of our very essence. It is indeed the simplest definition of honesty. Life is all of experience, all of emotion, pain and pleasure. By embracing the truth of our full experience, we arrive at the fullest expression of all that we are.

The seeking of the relief of pain is Universal. It is a fleeting, intermittent motivator of change. When the relief of pain is the primary goal, the motivation ceases upon such relief often **before** understanding is reached. It is also a common MYTH that pleasure only happens when pain is absent, removed, ignored or denied. WHAT IF? the avoidance or denial of pain to achieve pleasure or success is actually a barrier to success or pleasure? Many women report that removing or deadening the pain of delivery significantly negatively alters the overall experience of childbirth by creating a **barrier** to the overall pleasurable process of delivery.

Another example of the essential value of pain is in the disease of Syphilis. In one of it's final stages, Syphilis teaches us that pain and the ability of the body to register, respond to and respect pain is essential in preserving the body's natural state and function. In late stage Syphilis, damage to the pain receptor pathways of the spinal cord prevent the affected individual from adaptively managing the everyday minor injuries to the knee. Without the ability to recognize and respond to normal daily pain, the afflicted individual continues with repeated re-injuries and the joint over time is gradually destroyed.

Doubt and questioning are additional predictable hurdles to the Pilgrim's exposure to anything new. The intensity and magnitude of these elements exist to preserve the current state. We tell ourselves that our present circumstance is "safer" than any potentially negative results of change. Surprisingly, quite often current (imagined) personal security is preferred even though our situation may be one of acknowledged dissatisfaction. One is therefore introduced to the **power of fear of the unknown** as a basis for irrational, in the moment, easy, familiar choices.

Failure is a universally identified and misunderstood phenomenon which has much to teach us about its opposite—**success.** Failure is an integral part of growth and learning **not a sign of weakness.**

When an individual considers a new experience as one of the barriers to achieving, the possible goal assumes an inner tension, even fear, of what the outcome or the learning experience may produce—failure, disappointment or even unknown, unpredicted, and undesirable results. Anxiety to change is focusing on past resources or the "current" state irrespective of possible future "success." This element of learning is NORMAL and predictable and only becomes a barrier when the Pilgrim allows the uncomfortable experience of being anxious to define whether the pursuit of the goal continues. The single most significant barrier to successful learning is motivational and emotional NOT intellectual. Similarly, "Success Phobia" is actually a misnomer. It is more accurately "Change Phobia."

If you persist and are patient, the rewards of confronting these barriers to change will be self-understanding, personal respect and integrity. You will overcome the common and predictable NATURAL barriers to learning and acquire new information and understanding. By confronting your doubt, fear, and pain, **you will experience personal accessibility and awareness and an improved relationship with yourself.** You may experience a new understanding of what it means to **Focus**...to **Detach** from possessing... to accept **Loss**... to know **Fear.** You may discover that **Conflict** is not unwelcome... that **Creativity** is constant and that **Time** is all there is.

As you proceed, there will be times when you will, as we have discussed, become frustrated, confused, and perhaps even disheartened. DON'T DESPAIR. These experiences are natural and predictable elements of the process and NOT predictors of the outcome. Most Pilgrims benefit from the counsel of those who have gone before and from continuing to learn life's lessons deliberately and with great patience, particularly with themselves. If you follow the directions and suggestions herein and continue over time, you will find "The Recipe", the essential ingredients, steps and recommendations to exploring this book and yourself. **Successful journeying is primarily an EXPERIENTIAL process —not an intellectual one.** Those people who try to "think" their way through this experience as a "safe" or efficient way of exploring the content will only derive minimal benefit. Often dissatisfied people express interest and even expend huge amounts of energy and resources toward the pursuit of happiness while openly and knowingly not following the instructor's directions. When students subsequently "FAIL", they conclude that the reason for the Failure was either their lack of ability, the ineptness of the teacher, or the difficulty of the task.

You cannot read the first and last chapters of this resource and "Get It." As always, the tortoise actually does win! **WHAT IF?** being in a hurry, impulsive, and impatient are some of the cardinal components of the barriers to learning an alternative way? **WHAT IF?** "slow and deliberate" is actually the most efficient way of "getting it?"

Accompany those of us who have done and are doing this—learning, living and continued learning. When the going gets tough and it will, focusing on "WHY am I doing this?" and questioning the original intent or value of the pursuit will block your goal to achieve an alternative way of living. During the learning process when the experience becomes difficult, if the primary focus shifts from the learning to the adversity the learning process is halted. If you stop, you lose. Pausing, however, is an integral part of the learning. Ongoing pursuit maintains the gains and develops further learning. Journeying Pilgrims rarely ever come to me and ask, "Do I have a problem?" The individual who seeks her truth almost always knows something is "wrong." She is asking, "What can I do about it?" When she begins to learn, she also knows that Progress is happening. Few people ask, "Am I better?" Isn't TRUTH Wonderful! Success is an internal "bulls-eye!" There are many recurrent Human, Natural Truths that you will discover or, more likely, re-discover.

The work will, at times, feel lonely. As you develop personal presence and personal awareness, you will find that the lonely will gradually subside. It is the focusing on your feelings, your experience, and your self—FULLY—which quenches the thirst for attachment.

WHAT IF? the central ingredients in the discovery, maintenance and preservation of the individual's spirit are identical to those necessary for the human culture? The rules which govern individual emotional experience are the same as those which direct society. WHAT IF? safety, personal awareness, responsibility, honesty, motivation, and self-respect are different descriptors of the same issue—Life? Is it possible to be unsafe and unaware of one's self without knowing it? Who is more unsafe—someone who is unsafe and knows it or someone who is unsafe and does not know it? Do you want to know if you are "unsafe" and "unaware?" WHY? Will consequences of the lack of awareness occur if you do not know that you are unsafe? What happens if you just close your eyes and continue telling yourself that it is "OK" to cross the street now because you "want to" or "need to" and the traffic will miss you or that unprotected sex "this" time will not be a danger to you? Is it possible to be figuratively OR literally SUICIDAL if you are not thinking about killing yourself or your spirit?

How many people do you know whom you would describe as unhappy, unfocused, dissatisfied, unaware of themselves, poorly motivated, rarely creative, driven by external events, chasing or being chased by ideas, issues, individuals, insecurities, or other "external" events that will most likely be irrelevant to them in a "moment?" Are you one of these people? How about an alternative?

Directions

YOU MAY APPROACH THIS PROCESS IN ONE OF THREE WAYS. First, you may read the book in sequence completing the exercises as suggested. This choice allows the reader to move along with the book as a companion. Secondly, you may read Chapter 1 and then proceed with the exercises (Page 183) in sequence with the referenced chapters as a resource. This choice enhances the focus on the individual reader's experience as you explore yourself and the text. Thirdly, you may read the book in its entirety and then begin the Journal and exercises in the sequence suggested. This choice provides the reader an initial overview before self-exploration. The first and second choice will limit or reduce the number of potential distractions to your progress. Caveat—yes, even this book or a coach/therapist can in and of themselves, become distractions to you in your journey. Until you can recognize these or any distractions as a separate experience from your learning about yourself, you may become derailed by something you think you "should" be thinking or feeling. The simplest example of this process is illustrated by the all too frequent occurrence of the dependent student working with a coach or therapist to deal with the problem and becoming dependent upon the coach or therapist in the process. This is lateral movement and in as much as it requires detachment from the previous elements of dependence, it is a kind of growth. However, in the experience of this traveler, the lateral growth process is not nearly as efficient or productive as the experience of avoiding the lateral attachment during the learning process. **The goal is not to become "like" the teacher but to assimilate the lessons of the teacher as** enhancements of your own essence.

FINAL ADMONITIONS: The trip is best digested in a timely fashion, step by step and not responsive to the student's pressure or insistence at increasing the rate of uptake. Learn to be patient with yourself and to give time and nature a chance. WHAT IF? personal success (reaching your goal) is not something one "makes" happen but simply ALLOWS to occur? Only those who continue their self study will be able to adequately evaluate their choices in the end.

The process of change rests entirely upon the learning and full acceptance of all that you are and have been. One must then address one's experience openly and with patience and diligence. The extent of what you have missed and are missing will most assuredly astonish you on your journey. The magnitude of your surprise will only be exceeded by the quality and substance of the overall impact of your exploration.

May your journey be one of grace, open heart, and respect. Peace, Contentment, and Creativity Await You.

CHAPTER TWO

Beginning the Journey

*What lies behind us and what lies
before us are tiny matters compared
to what lies within us.*

– Ralph Waldo Emerson

History which is not known or understood is both lost and compelled for repetition. Entire civilizations of complexity and productivity have been lost, with the only surviving record available to date being a few pieces of pottery and a few cave or stone wall etchings. It is the advent of written history and recent generations' recordings of the richness of tribal culture of the Native Peoples that preserves only a small component of that complex and wonderful civilization. In the case of the individual, you will find as others have that your personal history is lost to you in the absence of such a record. You will discover how much of your own lost history will literally COME ALIVE simply as a result of direct reflection and attention!

Let us then begin by taking the first step on the path of your personal discovery journey—the path of your private and deeply sacred truth. The steps will be recorded daily for both development of your immediate awareness and as a testimony to those truths that walk with you daily but are inadvertently or purposely missed.

You are in the foyer of a Holy place, the temple that cradles your spirit. Let us begin.

You may complete the exercises as you read the text or you may proceed to the Exercise section (Page 183) and begin the exercises listed there following the directions in sequence as given. Each exercise will have frequent references to various chapters in the book and you may find yourself reviewing previously read sections as you proceed. Most students report that these "review" experiences of the text bring new insights at subsequent stages of personal discovery.

First Assignment

BEGIN BY COMPLETING:

Exercise One, Journaling, page 190

Purchase two blank journals, one to be used now and one later, and a wind-up "stove top cooking timer", color of your choice. As your coach, for the time being, I am asking for "5 and 5"—ten (10) minutes each day from you.

If you do not have ten minutes each day to invest in yourself and your future then you should not continue with this book until you do. Surprisingly, you will discover that finding even 10 minutes just for yourself may require an extraordinary effort—at least, in the beginning. Many of us go through our days completely concerned about everything in the world other than ourselves. Are you not at least curious what the outcome might be if you literally put your own experience at the top of your list of daily priorities? Can you name the things that you currently commit yourself to regularly without fail? Does your list include brushing your teeth, feeding your animals, or maybe taking out the garbage? Isn't it rather incredible that we fail to place the full exploration of our own spirit as a priority on a daily basis—not to mention moment to moment?

The pursuit of self-awareness is a priority and logically demands that we continuously explore and attend to the complete and full nature of our thoughts and feelings. We are unable to appreciate that which we are not attending to—our experience of life itself. Ask yourself. What percentage of my life's length to date have I allowed myself to embrace completely, moment-to-moment, without repression, rejection, denial, or some degree of restraint? WHAT IF? your life has been lessened by your attempts at "achieving", keeping up, satisfying others, or juggling all of the multitude of responsibilities that we all readily accept as the basic prerequisite for living instead of our ongoing personal enlightenment? Could it be possible to identify, sense, and express all of our experience moment-to-moment completely without neglecting essential survival elements such as paying the rent, mortgage, car payments, taxes, or tending to social responsibilities? WHAT IF? you have given up your spirit in the service of all that is outside of life itself? How many of us have assumed that savoring personal, emotional, and spiritual moments could be secondary to managing all of these "essential" survival pressures? How many people have you known who have achieved personal contentment and creativity without doing this?

*

What if?

finding self

is something

you simply

allow

to occur

*

As you read this book in the order and in the manner recommended in Chapter 1, separately and simultaneously begin or continue to keep a PERSONAL JOURNAL (see sample journal page, page 193.) Your journal is completely private and accessible to NO ONE. Some Pilgrims find the password protection available in many word processing programs a convenient method of insuring privacy. Spend a MINIMUM of 5 minutes in total solitude simply REFLECTING—WITHOUT WRITING OR RECORDING—what your preceding day was like for you in terms of your feelings AND thoughts. When you do this, you will SET THE TIMER! FIVE MINUTES! Do not exclude long term memories that come to mind as you explore your day in thought. Allow the thoughts and feelings to come in whatever form they take. NO MENTAL EDITING OR WITHHOLDING! When the timer goes off, your reflection is over unless you choose to continue. However, it is not recommended that "new students" exceed 30 minutes total time: reflection plus recording, 15 and 15.

Next, spend a MINIMUM of 5 minutes RECORDING in your journal the thoughts and feelings you have *just had* while writing your reflections. Do not read what you have written. The primary focus at this time is recording what your inner experience produces without assistance or distraction from any source.

Simply record the ideas and feeling that literally dance through your mind during the reflection period. You may be amazed at the complexity and flow that emerges once you open the door during the reflection. Do not be impeded or hesitant concerning the form of your recording. You may make your DAILY entries in any manner you choose, single words, sentences, or phrases (preferably not poetry.)

Any form that in YOUR opinion accurately depicts the reflection experience is the most desirable form. Even single words may suffice to pinpoint and establish a later accurate point of reference. The question that best serves the deliberate journalist is, "Will this record bring me back to the reflection when read at a later date?" One example of a simple recorded entry FOLLOWING REFLECTION might be:

Monday, July 29, 1996 @ 10 PM
5 Min Reflection, 5 min Recording

"Discouraged... depressed... tired... at times confused... still hopeful... The Journal may be helping... Today was unusually hectic. The work load at the office continues to increase, and I am quietly struggling with whether how I do my job is truly acceptable. I find myself, at times, more concerned about what others think of my performance than how I feel about it. I was so rushed this morning, I nearly ran a stop light. My daughter's birthday brings back memories of my own 16th birthday and the incredible complexity of my teen years. I think I am still struggling with some of the same feelings I had then. I find it hard to accept how difficult losing that last 10 pounds has been. I can't wait for our vacation in August. I so need a rest. Will there ever be enough time in the day? I realize how overwhelmed I sound. I feel discouraged and uncertain as to how to deal with all of this. I'm confused about how to change things. I'm aware of feeling sentimental and depressed. I feel old, I feel afraid. And, somehow I feel better admitting that! Ha! I can't believe me!"

The opportunity to learn from your entries as an enhancing experience will come later. Doing so now will contaminate the clarity of the focus on your "self" experience which is the foundation of self awareness. Yes, one CAN be distracted from awareness of one's self by one's own journal! The ability to learn from your journal contents will come later and will be even richer if the process of reviewing your reflections does not constitute a distraction from your ongoing commitment to maintain personal awareness AT ALL TIMES! You may go beyond 5 minutes and up to 30 minutes (REFLECTION AND RECORDING TOGETHER)—total. Access to professionals in your community and/or via the web site will serve as resources to you in your "travel" (Please refer to The Addendum). If you lengthen the Reflection and/or Recording Time, it is recommended that you do so by equal amounts in each category, preferably consistently. This is not intended to be a burden, but rather, an opportunity! (See Figure 1, page 41.)

Sample Journal Page

What are/were my feelings and thoughts today/yesterday?

What Is My Truth

Date: _____

Reflection Time: _____ Recording Time: _____

◆

Leave 2" margin

blank for later

additions, notations

& observations

◆

_____

_____

_____

_____

_____

_____

_____

_____

_____

_____

_____

_____

FIGURE ONE

Many are surprised at how difficult "beginning" the JOURNAL CAN be. I have seen some Pilgrims begin their personal journal by spending months to years just *thinking about* doing it as their first step. In order for this to be a first step, one must proceed to Step Two which would be the actual Reflection and Recording. Otherwise, the "thinking" about it becomes an avoidance and an end unto itself.

Remember, this process will take TIME in the pursuit and in the emergence of your awareness of the nature of the study and its evolving impact on you. You are exploring not only a new process but a new subject—YOURSELF! Be kind and steadfast as you go. Expect periods of resistance and the emergence of pain from current and past memories that may require care, consideration and compassion. It is not necessary to fully address all of each emotion and thought as they emerge if the journalist is willing to at least identify the discomfort or difficulty and note it within the journal. There will be ample time at a later date to allow the remainder of the discomfort to emerge through reflection and review of the entries. The essential component is to willingly include the painful content at the first level of identification.

How many times have you regretted not putting aside even a small amount of your earnings on a regular basis, say $100.00 over the years? What magnitude of resource would you have preserved for current use if you had done so? The same holds true for moments and memories you record in your JOURNAL! You will find that the reflection and recording process will not only have an immediate impact on your current self-**awareness**, but also on your overall self-**experience**, and like the financial metaphor, you will discover a kind of emotional savings account that actually does pay dividends. Many insist these resources grow exponentially.

Chapter Three

Who Are You? Who Am I?

Let Us Be Properly Introduced

All real living is meeting.

– Martin Buber

Please allow me the opportunity to introduce you and myself to you! We have many things in common and much to share. I have known you for many years as my neighbor, friend, spouse, child, mother, father, uncle, aunt, grandparent, relative, supporter, teacher, peer, teammate, student, and fellow traveler. I have been amazed, for longer than I am comfortable in acknowledging, how much both of us have either ignored or altogether missed the TRUTHS of our common experience along the way. My explanation for waiting until now to speak is fraught with procrastination and distraction by many previously experienced "higher priorities."

I am a messenger, not a creator. I am no more the "inventor" of the principles presented in this manual than Benjamin Franklin or Thomas A. Edison were of electricity or light. I am the eyes of the blind, the ears of the deaf, and the limbs of the lame. I am aware of the simplicity of the gift of life and the sacred and holy foundations of the human spirit. I am aware that there is a common dimension among those I have been privileged to assist and a uniformity in the process of healing that all Pilgrims share. I want to help you

◆

What if?

you don't

know what

self-respect

is

◆

to know and fully appreciate all that is the gift of life and all that you are. I am pleased that you are choosing to give the only truly valuable real estate in the universe—that of Life Time itself. Thank you for your gift. In return, I am blessed with the opportunity to share the wisdom offered to me by many learned travelers.

I am Pilgrim James Patrick Ware. I have been quietly practicing medicine (General Medicine, Child, Adolescent, Adult & Family Psychiatry) for nearly twenty-five years. I have lived for almost a half century, and I have worked with people professionally both on an individual and small group basis.

I have family of Welsh, Irish, Jewish and Cherokee origins with individuals of varied achievements including teaching, ordained ministry, manual labor, black smithing, medicine by horseback, petroleum production, and politics. My grandmother insisted for years that we were the ninth generation of cousins in the Father of our country's family! (Yes, old George W. himself.) I have found that over the years all of these influences have surfaced within my awareness demanding I honor and acknowledge their presence. I have become intensely aware of deeply ingrained personality and character traits which have direct roots in my ancestry. My love of nature, hard physical labor, spirituality, understanding, learning, civilized gentility, humanitarian passion, and creativity in any form are profoundly personal foundations of my experience which have become known to me through my own personal journey and discovery. These discoveries, for me, are graciously gratifying and satisfying.

I am reminded of my earliest experiences in awareness which began my personal journey. My early injury at age two, as previously mentioned, begins my log of experiences and my current conscious awareness, and thus constitutes the beginning of my developmental learning. Subsequent early experiences which surface include events around age 3-4 involving various elements of mischief and deception in play activities as strategies for postponing bedtime. Perhaps the most poignant early memory is a general sense of well-being and contentment which I later, around age 4-5, associated with the relationship I had with my mother and her intelligence and understanding of the many wonders of the world. At about age five, I recall playing at her feet as she ironed my father's starched work shirts and talked about her concern regarding the state of world tension and the threat of global war. The year was approximately 1952. She emphatically stated her belief that, "When Stalin dies, the world will be a safe place!" I instantly knew that there was no way that the death of any one man would constitute the basis for world peace as I then understood it. I was immediately aware that what had constituted my security, my calm and peaceful world, had been my mother's knowledge and overall capacity to "provide" for me. This was, in fact, not true. I realized I could not solely depend on my mother. I needed to seek other sources. My journey and my learning had just taken a giant leap forward. You may recall your first moments of learning and self awareness. This discovery when actively pursued yields more memory and even more current personal awareness.

The closer to and more complete with our experiences we are, the more respect we have for the quiet but ever-present cultural and genetic heritage carried within us. If we consider that all of mankind's history is embodied within the genetic codes laid down in our cells, it becomes truly an adventure of the mind to consider and conceptualize the untapped but ever-present information within these codes—a process that the most advanced laboratories are just beginning to unlock. We truly are the culmination of all who have gone before us.

I am your brother, son, father, student, co-worker, friend, uncle, and fellow traveler. We have spoken many times and, all too frequently, have each been focused on issues and elements of our surroundings and experiences which have kept us from truly knowing ourselves and one another. I am proposing to change that for you and for myself—as individuals and as fellow Pilgrims. I am aware of the multitude of barriers (personal, political, environmental, financial, organizational, and others) that exist for the average individual in accessing quality resources. I have been spurred to pursue the creation of this work by that knowledge and by other Pilgrims, both patients and colleagues. They have urged me to share the "lessons" offered in a readily available form as a tool to use toward self-awareness and personal development. I am looking forward to sharing these lessons with you and your sharing yours with me and others.

You have many incredible qualities and capabilities within you which I have admired for many years. I have not fully understood until recently how it is that you have not fully utilized these abilities. As I have explored my own depths and experiences, I have been continually, silently aware of the profound "oneness" of the visible Truth within us which you and I have and may reach. It is incredible to me that so many of you seem, as I have seemed for many years, to intermittently search for understanding and at times gain certain pieces of the puzzle, only to at other times, appear not aware or even interested at all!

We seem entangled by the sense that "hard" or "painful"

are inherently harbingers of a negative or undesirable out-come. We appear to be "addicted", "attached intensely" may be a more accurate description, to taking the "easy" way in-the-moment overtly telling ourselves that we are "fine" and getting "the most" for our minimal effort. When we allow ourselves the luxury of simple self-reflection, which is rare due to its association with a sense of self-disrepute, we qui-etly know that we are postponing facing up to ourselves and our own personal Truth. Our self-appraisal is often only a partial truth and is usually comprised more of others' opin-ions rather than our own.

I am truly amazed by the ubiquity of natural characteris-tics in the reports of travelers who have elected to make their own journeys. Once committed, the overall experience of self-discovery ALWAYS has associated with it the acknowl-edgment that the traveler has often "suspected" the truths she is discovering but has "put off" their use. This disclosure usually is accompanied by multiple expressions of embar-rassment, sadness and pleasure. Often, we regret not having begun the journey earlier in life. This momentary pause for acknowledgment is, however, usually very brief. The traveler is now struck by being immediately compelled to actively pursue further self-exploration with intensity and a full investment of energy and creativity without regard to periph-eral constraints, including the lack of time.

With few exceptions, perhaps none, I am aware that you have a depth of ability and passion for life and its fullness that cries out for release and expression! The pathway of discovery is the same for each of you, including initial steps, falterings, acquisitions and finally the expressions of your completeness. Let me continue to share with you those aspects of your person which I have noted as I have been

♦

What if?

you've

lost

"it"

- you

♦

with you these many years.

You may have for most, if not all, of your recalled life been dissatisfied with your overall experience in many ways, including but NOT limited to, your sense of well being, contentment, self-respect, creativity, self-confidence, intimacy, courage, perseverance, and overall personal solidarity. Additionally, many of you initially have significant difficulty taking yourselves back to your past. You have looked for the "answers" in many other places. You have approached me and others on many occasions and attempted to get us to "agree" with you in some respect, hoping that acquiring our concurrence on some idea would bolster or establish your truth, identity, self-awareness, and self-esteem.

You may have quietly seen others as having achieved these goals because of abilities or advantages you do not feel you have or, perhaps, you have pessimistically accepted that the successes presented by others are actually unreal, mere stage presentations with no basis in TRUTH. You have attempted to mimic things you have seen others do in hopes that the success **you think they are having** will "rub off" on you if you duplicate their behaviors. You wear the clothes, speak the language, and attempt to recreate the general postures of "success" in manner, attitude and possessions in an attempt to create WITHIN the experience that you seek from WITHOUT!

You have exhibited an **unbelievable ability to ignore your own false sense of inadequacy** which quietly has perpetuated your denial or pressured attempts to complete yourself. The inner experience of emptiness when allowed to surface, even if only briefly, is accepted as incontrovertible evidence of the need to acquire "something" or "someone" that you do not have.

The nature of the barriers that repeatedly sit in guard of your discovery of your TRUTH are relatively simple although you experience them in most cases as prohibitive. When you discover the full nature of the barriers and challenge them, you will predictably succeed in your own pursuit, as well as emerge as a teacher by virtue of your inner drive — WITHOUT EXCEPTION!

Second Assignment

BEGIN NOW BY COMPLETING:

Exercise Two: My Earliest Awareness, page 195

Exercise Three: Initial Self-Appraisal, page 196

Exercise Four: Personal Change (optional), page 198

Exercise Twelve: Personal Daily Schedule, page 209

CHAPTER FOUR

On
Becoming
Aware

Learning
About
Learning

A man cannot be comfortable

without his own approval.

~ Mark Twain

There are few experiences in life as intense and stimulating as learning and mastering something altogether new. The process is experientially a virtual recapitulation of all that we ARE or in some cases, all that we ARE NOT! This you will see as this resource and you unfold together. Understanding the basics of the learning process is essential in maximizing the efficiency of the learning of a particular subject. Many take the learning process for granted which results in either a burdened, complex, problematic learning experience or end result or both.

In an attempt to be complete and not exclude any essential components of this presentation, let us presume at this time that you are unaware of the learning basics. Let me encourage you to be open to ideas that you may initially consider to already exist in your "tool" box. It is not uncommon that students on this journey find in the end that they have learned as much about learning as they have about themselves. Don't cheat yourself and assume you already **know it all!** Be patient and proceed along the steps recommended, allowing this reference and the suggestions to introduce you to aspects of learning and yourself that you may either not be aware of at all or are not using to their full potential.

Third Assignment

COMPLETE NOW:

Exercise Five: Prior Learning & Achievement List, Page 199

Exercise Six: Self Awareness Pursuits, Page 200

Let me again remind you that this reference is intended as a catalyst and introductory vehicle—a kind of written personal coach. The essence of the lessons will emerge from your own awareness in thought AND feelings over time. You will find that this learning process will mature and become more sophisticated as you continue and literally learn HOW TO LEARN about yourself.

One first time Pilgrim described his initial experience as follows:

> "I've never done a personal journal...never known anyone who did...it's out of the mainstream...to keep a diary...not a normal "human" thing to do...I'd think that would be unusual, weird, undesirable...even if everyone did it, it would still be difficult for me to do...I don't think I want a historical record of all of my thoughts...they are private...no one else's business...It's

*awkward...I'm learning things, too...it's enlighten-
ing...it's exciting...encouraging...to learn something
about myself I never thought about or to hear answers
to questions you would never ask yourself...I wouldn't
have asked those questions myself...the idea that I have
thoughts and feelings that I just don't pay attention to
or am not aware of moment-to-moment is unbelievable...there are parts of me I truly don't know...unless I
looked...I wouldn't have asked the questions and
wouldn't have accessed more...I wouldn't have had the
experience of learning about myself things that are
there and I'm not aware of...I came wondering if it
could even happen... I'm exhausted...I've spent thou-
sands of unproductive dollars over the years...without
motivation...I'm exhilarated...it's focus, consideration,
experience, then...exhilaration...I wonder what percentage of the world knows how to do this...it's very
small, I think...a few percent...it's a motivation factor...
other people need to know ..."*

You are by now simultaneously "tracking" both retrospectively and currently several variables, namely your thoughts,
your feelings and the suggestions (road map) recommended
in the exercises. Don't impede the "data" registry: don't edit,
qualify or judge the content AT ANY TIME! Let the information stand on its own. When you do find yourself editing,
judging or even excluding current and/or past thoughts and
feelings, don't judge that event. You WILL do it many times.
Consider this as a distraction from the process itself and note
it—much like a footnote in a text. Eventually, these "foot-
notes" concerning issues, memories and experiences you
find difficult to access, experience and explore will provide
a very informative road map in their own right.

One of the most important aspects of learning is the basic need for a simple awareness of the subject to be explored. In this case we are referring to an individual's awareness of herself. It is rarely acknowledged that many people literally do not "know" themselves. For example, the most common presentation in my practice as a therapist is an individual who initially indicates he "is" self-aware but is having some difficulty with a particular aspect of his awareness or experience—usually some element of pain or stress management. As the helping process unfolds, it becomes apparent as the various elements of self-awareness surface that you will learn many things about yourself that were outside of your immediate awareness and thus, were not attended to.

One such Pilgrim described her initial experiences with early self-awareness in the following manner:

> "I've been thinking about whether it was possible to have a relationship by yourself...I've thought about it...you can't make a relationship with just one person...there have to be two people...involved...not one...I know it's true...I've been missing something through my whole marriage...me...I felt that way...before I was 20...I never felt I fit in, like the black sheep...like no one ever wanted me...like I was different from...my whole family...that it was bad to be different from my family...I tried to journal...I put down the same old thing...every day...I'm probably not happy with who I am...probably not sure who I am...I lay guilt on myself, trying to be good...to please others...I'm tired of pleasing others... I'm not sure if I'm happy with me...I guess I'm not that happy with who I am...I want something for

me...to be something for myself...don't want to depend on others...don't want someone else to make me happy...I don't know who I am...I live my life totally trying to please other people...I definitely want to find me...always been someone else's wife or daughter...I'm sure I'm the only resistance...now I see it hasn't been about me...in the journal, it's been about others...not my feelings...it was always about everyone else...but, I thought, 'it's about me...not them'...If I can't be me...I can't be anything to anyone...it bothers me that I'm 40 years old and don't know what I want...but, I know this is real...so far...it totally makes sense to me...this is something different. I'm having the hardest time with the journal...why can't I do this...it's really hard...I ought to be able to do this...do I know myself?...no, I don't...I understand that it isn't possible to respect someone you don't know...me...this ought to be easier than it is...the first part does feel tough...it's my whole life...not validated...as to how I feel...I've always been put off...I guess I'm afraid...part of me can believe...this is real...that it could be...eventually easier and better...like learning how to do anything...it's harder at first...then...after you learn how...the actual doing is easy when you do it...you just use what you know...but it's hard to imagine doing that with me...."

The student usually discovers through persistent self-focus not only elements of the learning process itself, but aspects of herself with which she was not initially completely in touch. Many describe the experience as similar to getting to know someone they have never met. And, despite what may frequently be emotional pain as the new information unfolds, the student reports a central pleasure from the enhanced self-awareness and emotional release. Following this learning experience quite often there comes a disclosure by the new Pilgrim concerning these awarenesses. At this time, the coach or therapist has license to invite the student to further explore the possibility that there is much more to learn.

The basic foundation for the lack of awareness is most often composed of at least two elements. The first and most prominent is the desire to avoid uncomfortable feelings, memories or perhaps personality traits that are unacceptable to the student or more often to those close to him. The second is a tendency for people to look outside of themselves for relief of their distress or conflicts or gratification of their drives. The avoidance of discomfort is commonly accompanied by a simple drive to "do it the easy (painless) way." The universal myth herein is that "painless" is better. You will eventually discover that this avoidance of pain is one of the natural barriers of the common approach to managing stress that is pervasively counterproductive. **The desire to avoid discomfort and the tendency to look outside one's self for answers have in common the absence of focus on the individual student's own experience—for different reasons.**

The lesson is relatively simple. If the student does not (metaphorically) actually concentrate on the Algebra homework, the homework does not get done and the learning doesn't happen. In this case, the individual's own experience is avoided or omitted, conceptually setting the stage for an inner experience of "emptiness" or inadequacy. The individual misreads the experience as evidence of a personal "reality" often perceived as "unchangeable." It is as if the mind "reads" only the absence of experience or coping capacity and, as a result of the primary lack of personal focus for WHATEVER reason, does not readily associate the lack of focus with the inner experience of emptiness or inadequacy. Almost all new students are puzzled or UNCERTAIN as to the origins of their inner experience of emptiness or inadequacy. The student then simply responds to her sense of "can't," or ineptitude, and further looks to the periphery or outside for relief or answers, further magnifying the original focus problem, as well as the extent of the perceived problem! After all, the reasoning goes, if it feels broken, it probably is broken! If you look once for your car keys and do not find them where you thought you left them, then why look again?—or why not—"look again?"

Another early Pilgrim described her experience in this way:

"I am brighter than I knew I was...success is easier than I thought it was...you never know until you do it...easier and better...it's exciting...I felt at first, 'I can't...I felt totally stuck, useless, and helpless...I didn't know I wasn't...I gave up over and over and yet kept coming back...that urgency I had to do this...I couldn't believe it could be different and couldn't imagine it could be easier...I sure did think that taking care of yourself was selfish...I have so many things I want to do...I really know myself better every day...yes, it's just me...that I am a person and I count...that is the progress...you can't respect someone you don't know...before, I didn't respect myself...I didn't know who I was...I'm finding out I don't have anything...without self-respect...I'm working on not letting anything get between me and my journal...my distractions are when I stop thinking of me...like confrontations with family."

•

What if?

discovery of

self is

simply

learning

how to

learn

•

We will see in time why you should "look again!" Pilgrims describe feeling lost, ungrounded, and empty and intensely perceive themselves as without the internal substance to manage their experiences. What a surprise it almost always becomes when they discover that what was experienced as missing or impaired is actually "not in use!" At this point, the primary battle is entirely **within the Pilgrim** in terms of whether you continue mobilizing the MOTIVATION and COURAGE to pursue a focus on **yourself**—rather than everything or everyone else. It can be very difficult even with the initial positive experience described herein to encourage continued self-searching when the process is primarily painful or threatens current relationships. This is discussed in **Chapter Five on Attachment.**

Motivation is more important than ability. It is clear at this juncture that continuation of the process of self-study is the essential component of continued discovery (and uncovery) and further success. Those individuals who pursue with effort, patience and courage are destined, as in any other field, to end up with the "degree"...in this case, a more complete awareness of self. Do not prejudge the overall outcome based upon the current, qualitative experience. **Yes, No Pain, No Gain!**

When asked to reflect comparatively on their current vs past experience, Pilgrims at this stage begin to describe a gradually increasing sense of self, self-esteem, mood, concentration, general energy, motivation, socialization, and self-respect to name only a few of the internally changing variables. The emotional aspects of relationships are also changing. People describe fewer conflicts with others and an enhanced ability to more comfortably say "no" to significant others. A relative sense of freedom and choice emerges which, for the student, is CLEARLY associated with the degree to which she has focused on feelings and thoughts (past and present) and has "allowed" those feelings to "be" without contamination, distortion, denial, avoidance or repression. The student describes a general sense of calm, contentment, and enhanced freedom—often beginning new pursuits or resurrecting old pastimes or interests previously abandoned. One Pilgrim's husband exclaimed at this stage in the process that he was falling more in love with her "now" than when he first met her. An artist is born!

The basics of the Learning Recipe include the ability and willingness to be **open, accessible, attentive, patient, under-standing of apparent disappointments and/or expectations, non-judgmental, motivated, and focused. Furthermore, the ability to explore, to use repetition, and to have the courage to allow change** is critical. To be able to let go of "old" concepts and ideas, at least temporarily, is foundational to your pursuit. Additionally, being aware of the relationship of learning to the **attachment/loss** process discussed later in **Chapters 5 and 6** and having the ability to travail within the unknown, acknowledge your **fear, Chapter 7,** and allowing it to happen without impeding your **focus, Chapters 8 and 9, require direction** and **persistence.** In time, you will discover either via current reflection or periodic historic reflection that you are developing an enhanced ability to identify and experience more and more of your **total** experience including the pain. Concurrent improvement in your mood, sense of solidarity, and contentment begin to emerge as you spontaneously master both the processes of reflection and experience in and of themselves.

You will discover that certain elements of peripheral structure, things outside yourself, will either be supportive

(e.g., coach or therapist, the JOURNAL, supportive relationships with fellow Pilgrims, etc.) **of your endeavor or, if
allowed, will be DISTRACTIONS** (family and/or financial
responsibilities, dependent relationships demanding your
attention, and/or illness) **to your purpose. CONTINUE
FOCUSING ON YOUR THOUGHTS and FEELINGS BOTH
NOW AND HISTORICALLY.** Peripheral elements are, as you
will find, not inherently "good" or "bad" influences. It is how
YOU address them. You can choose to use peripheral elements to spur you on, remind you of your personal commitment and facilitate your "weak" moments as you go.

It is central to the process that you be aware as you proceed whether your focus is driven internally (by YOU) or
externally (by anything or anyone outside of you.) Be aware
that you will unconsciously exclude certain usually painful
memories, choices, relationships, challenges and/or experiences by nature and that tracking your sense of whether you
are being thoroughly "honest" with yourself in terms of
allowing ALL of your experience to surface unencumbered
is very important. Don't forget to remind yourself that it is
NORMAL to be inclined to AVOID unpleasant experiences—
just don't do it! YOU HAVE A CHOICE. You may from time
to time find yourself questioning the acceptability or validity
of your experience. REMEMBER THE GOAL is to allow yourself the privilege of having YOUR experience without judgement. You may also find yourself selectively omitting certain
ideas, memories, and experiences from your exploration.
DON'T EXCLUDE—JUST ALLOW THE EXPERIENCE TO
EMERGE.

Monitor your **FOCUS (Chapters 8 and 9)** as your PRIMARY
GOAL, remembering that **LOSS OF FOCUS IS A NORMAL**
part of the learning process and NOT an indication of **FAIL-**

URE. You will learn as much from the nature of your **LOSS OF FOCUS** as you will from the **MAINTENANCE OF FOCUS** as you explore an alternative way of living and dealing with life's experiences.

Be aware that your reflections will include both ideas and feelings and it is the PRIMARY GOAL to **ALLOW THE FEELINGS TO EMERGE**. This is much more taxing than reviewing and reflecting on ideas alone. Finding yourself immersed in primarily ideas is NORMAL and PREDICTABLE. It is a form of partial internal distraction. DON'T ALLOW YOURSELF THE EASY WAY OUT. Remind yourself of your commitment to yourself and the primacy of your experience without judgement and that the "easy" way is a kind of internal seduction in-the-moment. As you proceed over time, you will discover the TRUTH about "EASY." But, at this point, what FEELS easy is not, and you are NOT ready to evaluate the whole picture yet.

The discovery within yourself that you have certain unconscious expectations (for example, that the understanding of oneself is not necessary or it should come without effort) is a foreseeable event which many find embarrassing or difficult to accept in themselves. Remember to be accepting as it emerges; just do not let this internal distraction derail you. It, too, is a part of the process.

Often the perception of a particular trait (e.g., selfishness vs independence, stubbornness vs perseverance) is "in the eyes of the beholder." It is very common to meet individuals who readily acknowledge their intrinsic, often intense, resistance to change owning to "stubbornness." These same people, however, may respond in the negative when asked if they have the ability to persevere. However, I would like to suggest that these two personality traits are actually dif-

•

*What if?
the last
real frontier
is your
own spirit*

•

◆

What if?

you have

choices

you don't

even know

you have

◆

ferent sides of the same coin. The first deals with resistance to change and the second frequently deals with the pursuit of a goal (something new.) In essence, if you have the ability to be "stubborn," you have the ability to "persevere." You will eventually discover that the emotional efficiency of stubbornness is much less than that of perseverance; it is harder and less productive. That lesson, too, will have to emerge on its own.

It has also been my experience that students who EXPECT success usually achieve it. So, monitor your expectations as you proceed. The internal sense of purpose and expectation of outcome can, in and of itself, become an ally in times that may become tough. Namely, "If others can do this, why can't I?"

You must acknowledge your internal resistance to achieving your goal. This is a natural component and an element always present in the learning of something new. It is not unlike meeting someone new and having an initial anticipation of a new relationship only to be surprised "again" that the actual negotiation of the new relationship has a downside in some respect to which you are not attracted or motivated to deal with. This resistance must be embraced, not abandoned; it is not a sign of weakness or ineptness and has NOTHING to do with outcome—unless the Pilgrim ceases the process. The Journey which you are about is a multilevel experiential (not simply intellectual) learning experience that is SLOW, GRADUAL and dependent upon diligence, focus, experience, reflection, and allowing the experience to define itself.

At this point on your journey, it is important to make initial personal notes in your JOURNAL concerning your current and past experiences in certain categories for identification, monitoring and later, comparisons. These categories include (but are not limited to) quality of your mood, concentration, energy, motivation, pleasure, satisfaction, creativity, and intimacy. It is not unusual for a student who has progressed to a heightened quality of personal awareness to later discover that, on further reflection, his initial genuine personal evaluation was understated or undervalued in magnitude or in some cases, even denied altogether. For now, you should be satisfied with simply recording your awareness of these areas with whatever qualifiers seem most appropriate (e.g., very depressed for years, poor concentration, fair energy and motivation for select goals, etc.) Please refer to **Exercise Three, Exercise Section, page 196.**

As you develop your capacity to be more in touch with your experience, be painfully aware of any internal inclination to consciously understate or overstate the item. This is "DISHONESTY" and a foundational flaw in the success of your eventual outcome. Confront it, face it, and note EXACTLY what your TRUE experience is, as well as the tendency to misstate or **disown** the issue(s) or feelings and thoughts. You will learn more from this phenomenon later. Your willingness to COOPERATE with these directions is essential to your success. **To date, every Pilgrim I have worked with who has persisted has succeeded.** Remember, the initial stages of learning anything new are the most difficult. Learning a new language is initially much more difficult than speaking the language once you become "fluent." YOU WILL GET THERE!

Many students report an initial anxiety concerning getting to know themselves, not unlike having a "blind date." Remember, be honest with yourself and face the **TRUTH WITHIN** despite the, at times, intense resistance or reluctance. It is easier to focus on the possible negative outcomes or the unpleasantness of the current work or the actual feelings themselves than it is to allow these experiences to simply occur. Note their content and quality and CONTINUE ON!

In time, you will begin to "see through the fog"; do not allow yourself disappointment as an end point. The "vision" will come eventually without effort. If you find you are "pushing" the outcome or are impatient, you are distracted. Deal with it! If it has occurred to you that "Focus" and "Responsibility" are connected in this endeavor, you have just acknowledged that you are a reluctant Pilgrim! Welcome!

An inherent conflict exists between learning and creativity. Learning's basis is in structure and outside/external stimuli; creativity's basis is in movement away/separation from outside stimuli (issues/facts/structure.) The successful student not only allows new external facts in, but realizes the learning process is based on them. In this sense, the content of this book is actually "peripheral" to you, the student, and as such, is intended as an introductory vehicle for you to "meet" yourself. It is not meant to be used as a distraction or a basis for you to compare yourself with others. If you do this, you are misapplying this resource in the worst possible way. Do NOT compare yourself with external references, INCLUDING THIS RESOURCE.

It is critical to delineate the differences between the steps, stages, and content elements of the process of learning about yourself that are presented by this guide, including the predictions concerning the outcome(s) of your study based on former Pilgrims' experiences and the nature, quality and substance of your own personal data. In pure concept, creativity by definition finds its foundation upon movement away from existing or current status data. The primary data for learning in the creative paradigm comes from the unique feelings and thoughts and experiences of the individual Pilgrim (YOU)—not the content of this resource or these recommended exercises. This resource is intended only as a facilitator of your access to your own private unique reality and the origin of your creativity. You should not attempt to define yourself by the content of this offering.

You will find that there are elements of learning that are just outside of the awareness (subliminal.) At unexpected times, the Pilgrim will become aware of benefits, progress, and enhanced self-awareness and learning that truly have been ongoing although not directly within the awareness of the Searcher. These experiences will come from retroflection, current experience, and changes. This is not unlike the acquisition of the ability to "think" in a foreign language—from the first word learned to the moment that the student becomes "aware" that she is no longer translating, say from French to English, each time she communicates, but that she simply expresses and understands "the French."

Be PATIENT, FOCUSED, AWARE, DILIGENT, NON-JUDGMENTAL, OPEN, PERSEVERANT, ENDURING, AND CONTINUE ON.

We, those that have gone before you, are waiting with reverence and respect.

CHAPTER FIVE

Understanding Attachment

It is easier for a camel to go through the eye of a needle, than for a rich man to enter into the kingdom of God.

– Holy Bible (King James ver.), Matthew 19:24

Fourth Assignment

PLEASE COMPLETE:

Exercise Seven, Personal Attachment List, Page 201

Attachment may indeed be the "FORCE" that drives the Universe. These forces include the acquisition of money, power, control over others, land, title, etc. How much of this remains essential at the moment of DEATH? It has been said, "You can't take it with you." Is there not an implicit denial in the all too often pursuit of "things" in the face of our mortality? I am reminded of the familiar statement, "He who dies with the most toys wins!" Does this not raise the question of what is really important? Have people ever **"lost"** themselves in the pursuit of "acquisition" or, perhaps, simply in the process of attachment to others/things as found in relationships—"I can't live without him, her or it!"

Let us explore the natural history of attachment. If one explores early childhood development, acknowledged data documents the nature and evolution of attachment in the human infant. The process evolves, if unimpeded, through well-known stages beginning with separateness, proceeding through joining and on to fusion, with ultimate return to separateness, usually with great effort on the part of both the mother and the infant. It is not at all uncommon for the infant to actually perform better than the mother in this process. The process follows certain predictable stages whether the object to which the individual is "becoming attached" is animate or inanimate. How many of us have "missed" our favorite sweater or suit after we or our partner cleaned out the closet? How many of us remember the "newness" of our old car when it was first acquired? Do you remember the point when the "new" car became "old" in your awareness? The process is slow and gradual and in-the-moment, mostly imperceptible.

The process of joining or attachment is associated with an initial experience of separateness and, in the case of relationships or other objects, is usually the moment of greatest attraction. Subsequently, the joining transpires and the object becomes less new or even old. It is now known. Usually, quietly, the object becomes a part of the legion of things we experience as "belonging to" us or even "a part of" us, and when anything presents an implied threat to the status (separation or loss) of the object, we usually react with resistance

♦

*What if?
slow and
deliberate is
the most
efficient way
of getting "it"*

♦

as though we were having our own existence threatened! We have, at that moment, functioned "as if" we as individuals were one with the object.

Those of us who have experienced the development of intense, close, personal relationships that have changed or ended as a result of situations outside of our control can recall the inner experience of alarm and deep despair at the outset of the loss followed by a predictable sequence of events well-known to all—denial, anxiety, depression, and eventual acceptance—yes, separation. A graphic representation of this process involving two individuals may be seen here. (See Figure 2, below)

FIGURE TWO

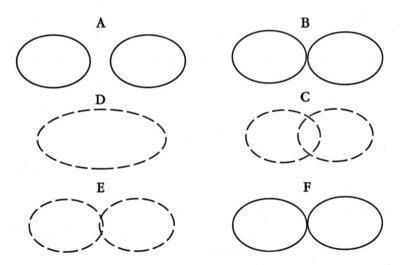

Two Individual Object Attachment Sequence

The individual's experience of a joined object (Figure 2-D) after attachment is commonly thought of as being "a part of" or even **equivalent to** the individual alone, emotionally. This joined identity is one basis for understanding the foundations for what many people use to determine their moment-to-moment experience. The individual may experience the object as equivalent to himself. When a person is joined with another object, the status of the connection and the object itself is often used by or perceived by the person in determining their sense of well-being, solidarity, security and contentment. People react to "threats" or perceived injuries/slights to attached objects as though the threat or slight was directed toward the person himself. If we explore all of the possible attachments for a generic person and give each item a relative value in terms of the importance the individual ascribes to each item, we have a kind of "attachment map" which can explain why individuals react (often unrealistically) when these attachments are threatened or eliminated. The first example below shows an individual with relatively equal investments emotionally with regard to Family, Job, Health, Recreation, Material Possessions, etc. In this case if any one of these areas were threatened or lost, there would be relatively less disruption of the individual's overall emotional sense of well-being than would occur with the second individual, who clearly values his relationship with one component much more than the others. A threatened loss of the partner in the second example would undoubtedly bring a catastrophic emotional response. (See Figure 3, page 77)

FIGURE THREE

FIRST
RELATIVELY EQUALLY BALANCED INDIVIDUAL
OBJECT ATTACHMENT PIE GRAPH

BALANCED ATTACHMENT

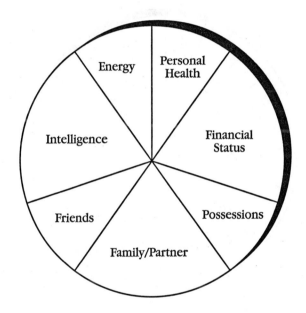

Personal Physical Health: 10%
Intelligence: 20%
Energy: 10%
Family/Partner: 20%
Friends: 10%
Financial Status: 20%
Possessions: 10%

FIGURE FOUR

SECOND
RELATIVELY UNBALANCED INDIVIDUAL
OBJECT ATTACHMENT PIE GRAPH

UNBALANCED ATTACHMENT

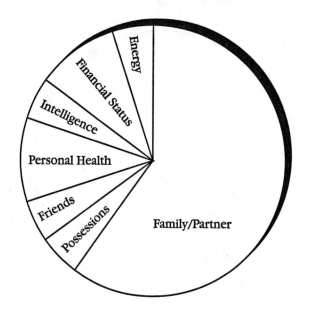

Personal Physical Health: 10%
Intelligence: 5%
Energy: 5%
Family/Partner: 60%
Friends: 5%
Financial Status: 10%
Possessions: 5%

We can see that as individuals we readily focus our emotional eye on external items and pay the price for not only the manner of the distribution of the investments but for the peripheral focus in and of itself. Imagine how a monastic member would react if he lost his sports car to thieves or natural disaster! We become the servants of our attachments usually without actually thinking about it. This is the prime basis for the advertising industry. Great research and effort go into understanding what factors enhance the rate, rapidity and quality of attachment an individual experiences with a proposed "new" item—in the sales vernacular, the "hook." Television commercials and ads are perhaps the best places to study the techniques employed by businesses to facilitate your connection/attachment with their product (e.g. sex, drama, color, shock, uniqueness, even offensive stimuli, in essence, anything that delineates the object as MEMORABLE!) Their goal is to establish in a fraction of a second, a connection between you and some element of their product which will produce a connection and hopefully, a sense that you "can't live without it," or at least a desire for acquisition. Some of these techniques are incredibly effective. What an "ART" form!

We now have one of the quiet lessons and one of the most important. Objects of attachment or, for our purposes, objects of distraction (things or people outside of yourself) may indeed be pleasant or unpleasant. In many ways, the pleasureful may be the most difficult to manage. That is probably why winning football coaches do "bed checks" the night before the big game!

Generally speaking, the intensity of the attachment predicts the extent to which the object operates as a distraction to the individual's maintenance of his self-awareness. A partner who understands that you MUST maintain yourself emotionally to be a part of the relationship is much easier to be attached to with minimal or no distraction than one who demands your undivided attention irrespective of your needs or circumstances. How often do you hear someone reflect on a close relationship that has been lost? At first, they didn't know how they would "go on" without their mate, only to later exclaim they never dreamed how wonderful life could be after they successfully negotiated the separation!

If an individual's response to the loss of a valued or "important" object is simply to "replace" the object with something or someone else, then their overall emotional economy will continue to be "dependent" upon the attachment stability. If, however, the individual directs the mind's eye or focus to themselves, there is an opportunity to achieve solidification or personal solidarity, which has an altogether different set of characteristics. As you explore your thoughts and feelings as outlined herein, you will find that this latter process will be enhanced. It is now appropriate for us to table further exploration of this issue until you have more experience with it.

It is apparent then, that the objects of attachment in our lives function, in the least, in powerful ways and that in the exploration of ourselves, they may indeed FUNCTION AS DISTRACTIONS! Let us explore just a few of the commonly highly valued attachments which are not (despite how you may be operating or what you may be telling yourself) **essential** to life itself.

fifth Assignment

Imagine yourself on a desert island or in a new world and simply list the things you would have to have to biologically survive.

DESERT ISLAND/NEW WORLD ESSENTIALS

_____

_____

_____

_____

_____

Sixth Assignment

Make a list of the top 10 emotionally significant attachments you now have.

_____   _____

_____   _____

_____   _____

_____   _____

Did you include in your list food, shelter, basic clothing, and water? It would not be unusual if your top 10 items either omit some or all of these essentials or include elements that are not only nonessential to biologic survival but would not be useable on a desert island. What if our emotional needs as individuals are metaphorically similar in their simplicity to our biologic necessities? How many of us confuse the many objects of attachment which have become emotionally important to us as emotionally necessary or central? How often do we see people valuing their Sunday ball game more than quiet time with themselves?

If tomorrow is the last day of your life, how will you spend it? Will you save some time to just reflect quietly on who you are and who you have been? Or, will you scurry about attempting to have more things or conversations with others? Many would leave themselves out of the day altogether or become so focused on what was going to be lost that they would miss what they have. Are we talking about you yet?

Ask yourself: What in the last ten years has been the most valuable time you have spent? Are you doing many of the same things now or are you distracted by issues, people, and events that will eventually, if not immediately, become empty for you? Have you ever had the experience of having "wasted" a percentage of your day, week, month, decade or life? You will have more of a sense of this question as we proceed.

Seventh Assignment

Please pick a time frame of a day, week, month, year or even decade and list the main areas of your endeavors and time investments. For example, consider how much energy you devote to attaining a certain financial status, possession acquisition, education, creative pursuits, relationships with others, etc.

TIME FRAME - Day, Week, Month, Year, or Decade
TIME INVESTMENTS - Please include percentages of total

Example: *Significant other-4 hours/day (16%)*

_____	_____
_____	_____
_____	_____
_____	_____
_____	_____
_____	_____

What are the simplest necessities of life? When you did the inventory of how you spent your last day, week, month, year, or decade, what percentage of the TIME invested would you consider as spent on ESSENTIAL subjects?

Is time spent on nonessential aspects of life "wasted?"

Have you ever experienced "losing yourself" in an activity, pursuit, or even relationship only to experience a tremendous sense of loss or letdown at the conclusion? Have you ever wondered in the end what in the world led you to "invest" yourself in such an item or person? Is it possible that your experience of loss of yourself has any connection to your having not tracked, maintained or even been aware of yourself during the time span of the "investment?" Is it then not only a sense of losing yourself but also of having lost time—your life time—in this process? This is a most essential point because, by implication, **SOMETHING THAT CAN BE LOST CAN BE FOUND!**

One of the most common exclamations of students who persist in the Pilgrim's way is that they feel "younger" and experience their days as being "longer" and much more productive. They emphatically state they feel as if they are manufacturing time or lengthening the days of their lives.

Attachment to peripheral objects is the antithesis of the Monastic life. Do Clerics know something about distraction and focus as they relate to the human spirit? Why are churches and libraries almost always "quiet" places? The drive to have, hold, and control defines the status of self as a function of things outside the self (REFERENTIAL.) Could this be the proverbial "Apple" of the Garden of Eden? Let us see! Can one misinterpret the experience of "apparent" well-being associated with stable object attachments as an indication of individual contentment? We resist the loss of these objects much as we would resist the loss of our life. As in business, success is a function of knowing when to "cut your losses"—OR is it in knowing where to "focus your attention?"

How much time and energy do we spend maintaining our attachment to those aspects which are agreeable but not central or critical to our personal identity? As you proceed, you will know more about this question AND be able to answer it easily. We seem to put great emphasis upon controlling variables in our world that are unessential to our own experience. Can the manipulation of others become an "opiate" of power and control within one's own identity? If so, this "power" personality foundation would then become a referential basis of identity and an intrinsic barrier against the full awareness of simple personal responsibility. It also replaces our feelings as a basis for self-esteem.

If one must establish and maintain focus upon and awareness of one's own feelings and thoughts irrespective of distractions, it would appear that *"responsibility"* for establishing and maintaining focus is a significant issue regarding how an individual is doing. We can easily see in the typical adolescent the pairings of avoidance of responsibility and the expectation that things will go well without effort; we in "the business" call that "entitlement." Do entitlement or avoidance of responsibility surface in age groups other than adolescence as potential barriers to success?

What would one label an object of attachment that is the self?

Would this be the proverbial and all-too-often elusive "self-respect?"

Does anyone Care about or Love Me? This question is unique to Humans. Imagine a young deer standing in the middle of a field demanding the hunter leave him alone! Only in the human do we see a kind of blind expectation that the environment will meet our needs without effort on our part. We have attached ourselves to many things, people, ideas, and experiences which have experientially become "us," and now in that attachment we are lost.

◆

What if?
you have
given up
your spirit
in the
service
of others

◆

One Pilgrim described this experience:

"I've always wanted to be dependent on someone or something...I've never really wanted to learn that I shouldn't do that...but, I guess, I've always known it...I guess it is the responsibility thing...the freedom thing...I thought it was possible to have what I wanted without responsibility...it's never worked...whenever I've gotten in...say, a relationship where the other person does everything, I say...the 'clingers'...it feels horrible, miserable, and... worse...then, I want out...I guess when I'm looking for an easy way...I don't think about the price of 'easy'...I do know now that looking for what I want by looking at getting it from other people just doesn't work...there really is only one person that the honeymoon doesn't end with...that's me. It's just hard to face the pain...to focus on myself...not on others, sometimes... but, it's the only thing that works...it really is self-destructive to avoid understanding and being aware of yourself...it's even 'suicidal' in some ways."

WHAT IF? Freedom, Liberty, and Creativity are indeed functions of our honest responsibility and focus? Let us continue on!

Eighth Assignment

COMPLETE PLEASE:

Exercise Seven, Personal Attachment List, Page 201

CHAPTER SIX

Understanding Loss

He who knows how to be poor

knows everything.

- Jules Michelet

Ninth Assignment

PLEASE REVIEW:

Exercise Seven, Personal Attachment List, Page 201

Review the list of all of the "things," people, abilities, resources in your life that you consider important to you and rate each one by percentage of its respective emotional importance (e.g., Personal Physical Health: 10%, Intelligence: 20%, Energy: 10%, Family/Spouse: 20%, Friends: 10%, Financial Status: 20%, Tangible Objects such as home, car: 10%, etc.) (See Figure 5, page 90)

Personal Attachment List

_____   _____

_____   _____

_____   _____

_____   _____

_____   _____

_____   _____

FIGURE FIVE

SUGGESTED CATEGORIES

Partner: _____%

Health: _____%

Intelligence: _____%

Possessions/Assets: _____%

Job/Vocation: _____%

Financial Standing: _____%

Debts: _____%

Other:

                    _____%

                    _____%

                    _____%

                    _____%

                    _____%

                    _____%

Make your own
PIE GRAPH

Be sure to use percentages that HONESTLY feel correct for you. Do not put down what you think the numbers "should be." Now imagine losing any one of these elements altogether, and make a list of the responses you would anticipate having along with a modifier of your choosing (say, mild, moderate or severe.) Include a measure of how much time would be involved in your "working through" the loss (say, 6 weeks, months or years.) For example, one might experience reduced concentration, sadness and/or depression, anger, denial, social withdrawal or isolation, reduced motivation, and/or decreased efficiency in productivity. You may choose to recall the loss of a valued item, person or experience in your past that actually produced the above experiences. If you choose a past loss for this exercise, it should be one that you have completed and thoroughly "worked through." If you have NOT actually worked through such a loss, then make your best estimate of the nature and substance of an anticipated loss experience that you either expect or are willing to allow yourself to imagine. Can you see that even the idea of **anticipating** an important "object" loss is a significant experience that takes energy, focus, and determination to experience?

The loss or anticipation of the loss of attached objects produces an emotional response similar to the reality "as if" the loss was of the person himself (a possible rehearsal for the loss of spirit itself?) The magnitude and nature of the impact is proportional to the extent that the individual has been defined by the attachment (e.g., the common story of an octogenarian dying shortly after the untimely death of a spouse for unknown reasons—a sympathetic death.) It would certainly make "sense" to avoid this experience, the pain of loss—or would it? Remember, keep your mind open.

Tenth Assignment

PLEASE NOW COMPLETE:

Exercise Eight, Personal Change/Loss Response Indicators, Page 202

The actual loss of a valued object is usually an unavoidable emotional event which "undresses" the prior existing denial of self-focus as the primary reality. Frequently, people attempt to deny the loss itself and, of course, most often "depression" is a visible consequence as associated with that avoidance. Isn't it interesting that we seem to "get" some of the puzzle pieces without much distortion and miss some or many of the others? Almost everyone that I have worked with agrees that when they are able to understand **experientially** the process of "letting go," depression improves dramatically or completely goes away. This understanding comes as you explore your full experience. The individual experiences sadness and grief which are clearly reported as different and painful in a more immediate sense than that experienced as depression. Moreover, in-the-moment, students emotionally embrace a general sense of relief and productivity and, to that extent, quite predictably report an enhanced sense of personal strength and integrity.

It appears that two processes occur simultaneously. The first and most important is usually the student's enhanced self-awareness and focus. The second is the experiential awareness that the heretofore "essential" object is actually NOT essential and in this moment, the separation process evolves naturally. The primacy of the initial step—focusing on the self—allows the second step to emerge spontaneously. By developing an awareness of one's feelings and thoughts and by more fully developing a personal connection with the self, one builds "the foundation" before dealing with loss. The resulting emotional experience is invariably one of release and relief. The most common and **unexpected** result of allowing the letting go process to proceed unencumbered is the enhancement of a new quality of attachment to the previously perceived essential object. Many individuals exclaim that they knew "true" intimacy must exist and would be "better" than the previously known version; however, new Pilgrims are amazed at the simplicity and grandeur of the newly discovered experience of attachment "without strings!" The combination of intimacy and a sense of "freedom" is unique and globally satisfying. Personal satisfaction is no longer a function of what is happening with the attached object or the attachment itself. Most students express concurrent embarrassment and pride at their new accomplishment and ability. It is not a surprise here to see the spontaneous evolution of new creative pursuits and an increased energy and general excitement about the opportunities that life has to offer. Old burdens and barriers become memories which can be difficult to revive. In many cases, until the student achieves the ability to readily reproduce this experience at will, he is very resistant to doing so for fear of a "relapse" into the historic muck and mire of the swamp of dependence.

It has been observed by many Pilgrims who have gone before you that one does not really know oneself until the loss of some "object" (valued attachment—person, ability, relationship, health, financial or intellectual resource) occurs.

◆

What if? the avoidance of pain is the barrier to pleasure

◆

◆

What if?

in

understanding

loss one

experiences

attachment

◆

Clearly, and paradoxically, it is the attempted preservation of "sameness" or the prevention of loss that encumbers the individual and **prevents** the discovery of self! Thus, as a result of the loss, the individual actually has an enhanced sense of self! **Loss, therefore, is not only an essential experience to embrace and understand in the pursuit of knowing one's self, but it is as you probably already know, a potentially powerful barrier to the process.**

Loss is universally accepted as something to avoid—ONE OF THE PRIMARY ERRORS. If one accepts this premise either consciously or otherwise, then forward progress beyond the attachment process CANNOT proceed, and learning about the self separate from all of those elements of the "us plus" WILL NOT HAPPEN. The student then experiences herself as UNABLE to acquire the new information or thinks that the new information isn't there at all. You will find in time that this is actually NOT TRUE!

CHANGE comes about most readily when the focus of the process is mainly upon attachment, NOT loss. An individual finds the acquisition of new objects much easier to negotiate than allowing loss. As you further explore these two processes, you will come to appreciate how intermingled they are and how interdependent they are! For the present, it will be enough to simply know that the decision of whether to allow yourself the experience of full sadness and grief surrounding a loss is one with far-reaching implications—the full nature and essence of development and a capacity to GROW. Courageously facing WHATEVER emotional experiences occur along with willingly embracing the new feelings and thoughts that emerge in concert with the old memories that surface in the process of getting to know (attach) yourself in the fullest sense will support a central attachment experience. This will provide a positive platform from which to discover a simpler and more manageable DISCOVERY PROCESS rather than one based on primarily focusing on "why" letting go is hard, painful or necessary (the negative approach.) The ability to allow loss to unfold naturally and in its own right is enhanced significantly by the extent to which the person is continually able to embrace and attach himself to past and present emotional experiences that have and do exist within his conscious repertoire. Do you find yourself doubting? That's OK. That may change as you find the offering corresponding to and being congruent with your prior and existing experiences!

Let us continue on together as we address the substance of our feelings and thoughts. From time to time we will explore how we are doing with the dreaded "letting go!" **We are only interested in what works for you!** Will you be surprised if you discover that not only is your personal emotional experience NOT in fact, **unworkable,** but it is clearly **functional?** This concept is along the same lines as the idea that individuals have abilities you could "never" possess. You will later discover that while there are truly a number of people who have seemed to "get it" on their own, the majority of people either don't get it at all or get it the same way you are now getting it—**with great fear, effort and at times trepidation!**

CHAPTER SEVEN

The Nature of Fear

And I will show you something
different from either

Your shadow at morning
striding behind you

Or your shadow at evening
rising to meet you;

I will show you fear in a
handful of dust.

– T.S. Eliot, The Waste Land

Fear is usually understood as the experience of apprehension, concern, trepidation and/or anxiety which occurs when an individual's security or safety is threatened or perceived as being threatened. The experience is associated with a full biological, and physiological set of responses in addition to the emotional components which, in and of themselves, signal alarm and danger. These physical responses may include but are not limited to: rapid heartbeat, sweating, rapid breathing, a sense of not being able to "catch" your breath, difficulty swallowing or a sense of choking, restlessness, difficulty concentrating, a sense of impending doom, general anxiety, variable and/or multiple physical symptoms including enhanced awareness of any physical sensation or preexisting discomfort, and/or a fear of dying.

In the last few years, physicians have learned they can give specific medications to block physical expressions of fear which, in turn, decrease the individual's awareness of or perception of danger. In many cases, the body reacts to a perceived threat involuntarily and the physical reactions can, in and of themselves, be barriers to the person's ability to function. The best example of this is an individual about to give a speech or take a test who anticipates the fear response (rapid heart, perspiration, impaired concentration, stuttering, tremors, etc.), preventing her from functioning at her best level. In this case, a medication which specifically blocks the body's ability to produce the "fight or flight" alarm responses removes the untoward impact of those alarm responses thereby opening the door for enhanced function. WHAT IF? there is a way for an individual to "remove" the barrier of fear that may be associated with other perceived threats to the individual or her survival?

Change is generally perceived by an individual emotionally and experientially as though it were a loss or at least a stress. All of the rules of anticipation of loss and the threat to the security of the integrity and/or survival of the individual apply to ANY change—even that of "positive" changes (marriage, birth of a child, job promotion, etc.) All have the stress of loss in that the "status quo" is no longer true. The individual reacts predictably with anxiety, denial, anger, depression, and adjustment on some level. It is the inherent resistance to change that becomes a barrier in the process of learning because the shift from the current state to a new experience requires a "change" and a "shift" from what is now known to something that is currently "unknown," and all of the above emotional and experiential reactions will and do occur. When the individual allows the fear and/or anxiety to become decision platforms upon which a choice is made to AVOID the change or loss in the learning experience, then the individual intrinsically and internally **prevents herself** from actually exploring the "NEW" arena.

If the individual understands the normalcy and predictability of this internal resistance, she may not only prepare and handle it, but actually recognize it as a central and integral stage of learning and change. With this understanding, the fear and anxiety become less strange, foreign and frightening and then can simply become a "stage" in the process. A young football player or gymnast who understands that extreme muscle soreness, nausea and vomiting, and even severe personal physical injury are concurrent experiences of the athlete will handle the emergence of these experiences better than someone who has no idea that these are normal and predictable elements of that particular pursuit. We have then an opportunity to bring down another "barrier" to learning and to allow a fairly natural process to take place—namely, the attachment of the individual to something new. **One does not "make" learning happen, one allows it to occur!** WHAT IF? the initial perception that the uncertain Pilgrim has of not being able to achieve a goal of self-awareness is actually a process that he cannot "make" happen, but can only allow to happen? In essence, the

♦

What if?
you have not
experienced
all that
life has
to offer

♦

*

What if?

there is

no rank

among

pilgrims

*

process unfolds on its own when it is allowed to do so!

Let us explore one example of how fear can actually be counterproductive in the process of learning and how learning can actually be at a level within the person that escapes overt intellectual awareness. Do you remember when you first learned to ride a "two-wheeler" bicycle? This process and memory is golden in understanding not only more about the learning process itself, but in its implications for the immediate task at hand. For those of you who have not learned, for whatever reasons, to ride a bicycle, please consider any other new skill that you have acquired—say in learning how to "think" in a foreign language or express yourself using a musical instrument (including your own voice) and follow along the bicycle metaphor, substituting the appropriate stages as we go.

If you remember how you learned to ride a bike, you can probably, with a bit more effort, recall the stage **before** the learning when you did not know how and when you were, predictably, ambivalent concerning this new challenge. To pursue meant to put yourself in danger of physical injury and/or failure, while to reject the challenge meant to deprive yourself of the opportunities and pleasures that many of your peers, siblings and others were having right before your eyes! What a dilemma! You were probably afraid of falling, crashing, and wrecking your bike and yourself! It was OUT-OF-YOUR-AWARENESS-FORWARD-MOTION that most frightened you because it was forward motion that would produce the most feared accident, or so your unconscious mind, (the mind of the neophyte) told you. Most people when questioned carefully about this experience cannot tell you what they were initially afraid of other than falling or being hurt!

What makes a bike move forward? It is simply pushing the pedals! And pushing the pedals was exactly what you feared the most! Those of you who eventually learned to ride a bicycle learned, most likely outside of your awareness, that pushing the pedals was actually the process that allowed you to control the bike's direction! Control was a function of literally doing that which you feared the most—forward motion. Slowly, you discovered that the pedals' movement allowed you to steer the bicycle, and you became a "RIDER." With a bit of time and practice, you developed the ability to use the bike so well that you rarely thought much of the process of riding beyond the pleasure you experienced during it, save for the occasional wreck, most often when you would be DISTRACTED from the basic operation of the instrument!

"Look Ma, No Hands!" ...CRASH!

This set of variables in the learning of a fairly simple task allows us to explore and uncover some basic truths about learning and achievement which are very directly applicable to the task of understanding oneself. We will refer from time to time to your bike, saxophone, French book or teacher. For the time being, let it suffice to simply establish that fear of new experiences is normal and predictable and that the inability to do something is not synonymous with the inability to learn **how** to do something. That which we fear the most may actually be a crucial step in the learning of the skill that is perceived as hard or impossible to achieve. And, finally, the eventual ability of learning to do something that is initially perceived as "hard" or impossible to achieve is actually not only simple but virtually profoundly easier than both the experience of learning how and the anticipated degree of difficulty! "Talented" artists frequently agree that they have more respect for the "new" student and the amount of effort required to maintain the effort, focus and motivation to pursue a **new** ability than they have for the individual who is actively using previously acquired skills. It is easier to "think" in French after one learns how than it is to learn **how to** think or speak French! The novice looks at the experienced holder of the intended ability as a kind of "Guru," which further mystifies and makes the acquisition less achievable in the mind of the inexperienced student.

Why not come along, pay your novice dues and join the ranks of the "Practitioners of the Self!" We welcome, respect, and await you. You will know us by our unflinching availability to share our understanding with you, as you will, when *you* reach the first opportunity to teach someone what you have achieved! Don't be surprised if that happens BEFORE you anticipate it. It is not uncommon for students to be achieving at levels far in advance of their awareness because one of the pitfalls of **being** a novice is distraction by views of the future. This results in a reduced relative awareness of the nature and magnitude of the movement from the novice's position. Some people even forget until queried what it was like to NOT be able to ride a bike, speak in French or play their saxophone.

Once we have demystified the reality of the novice (the "I can't" position and the fear of the unknown) and experienced the impact of learning we can recognize *apparently* striking differences in people that previously appeared to be indications of inequality in the basic essence of the people themselves. The phenomenon of "Storm/Tornado Chasing" would appear to many lay individuals as an expression of some type of insanity or self-destructive instinct. If one, however, looks at the readily available "video" records available in recent years documenting these incredible natural events, one discovers there are basically two types of storm recorders. One is the individual who just happens to be in the storm's vicinity with a video recorder and the other is the professional storm/tornado chaser. The lay video usually is fraught with many expletives and expressions of terror and panic. The professional chaser video, however, is usually associated with a commentary which exudes pleasure, excitement, and achievement. One would conclude that the informational base of the latter group allows that group to experience the storm in a vastly different manner from the first. How many of us respond to the everyday experiences of life like the "lay" public respond to the tornado? What would life be like for us if, with adequate information, we were able to allow life to be an opportunity of experience and expression rather than a kind of never-ending threat to our security and/or survival?

One must then be aware that fear or the experience of a threat to one's survival is not inherently an opportunity to "fight or flight", but indeed may be an opportunity to EXPAND our experience and our abilities to explore ALL THAT LIFE HAS TO OFFER! Imagine not being controlled by our fear but simply recognizing that it is one among many of life's sensations!

CHAPTER EIGHT

Beginning
to Know,
Understand,
and focus
Upon
One's Self

And ye shall know the truth, and the truth
shall make you free.

– Holy Bible (King James ver.), John 8:32

Take a deep breath and begin with courage. You are about to enter the world of your unknown! WHAT IF? the trip is productive and wonderful beyond your greatest expectations? WHAT IF? THE YOU THAT YOU DO NOT KNOW IS ACTUALLY THE YOU THAT IS MISSING? Now comes the doubt! Your uncertainty is about this guide and yes, ultimately about you because it is you of whom we speak. You may not be able to believe this is possible, because you have tried it before (or so you have told yourself) and for some reason, the experience was intolerable and/or unsuccessful. How could it be that pursuing what is painful or disagreeable would be associated with a successful result? What if? you are wrong? Who loses if you have simply not proceeded in a manner that produces success and you do not explore a potential alternative?

This offering does not seek to "change" you, but instead to offer you a viable alternative to your current manner of functioning. If in the end you actually prefer your former method of living, be assured you may switch back simply and immediately at your discretion. Until then, consider that in the absence of an actual "choice," you are indeed a "puppet" of your own current life style of "choices."

How many times have you stood in front of the mirror and asked yourself, "Just who is that person?" or found yourself, usually with effort, pushing out of your awareness some aspect of your personality or even your physical attributes (e.g., your manipulation of another person, pursuing some element of taking the easy way out when you knew it was not the best choice in the long run for you, wishing you were someone else or perhaps even wishing you had never been born?) Is there evidence that we avoid the TRUTH about ourselves when what we know, think, feel or suspect is painful or involves some expenditure of energy or effort (e.g., cheating on an exam is easier, and studying would actually entail "more" effort; acknowledging we actually do have big ears or a weight problem?) Do we tell ourselves that the easy way in-the-moment is the best and fail to explore all of the facts (e.g., quitting school or dropping out of an endeavor when the "going" gets tough?) Do we reject or deny our personality traits that we find internally or externally, personally or socially unacceptable and proceed on as though "nothing ever happened?" Or, worse yet, do we simply tell ourselves that reality is what we wish it was! Do we define "wrong" for ourselves as "when we get caught?" Do we expect, or even demand, an honest and responsible position FROM OTHERS while we endeavor to get by with the easy or most expeditious way? When was the last time that you looked for a family physician or surgeon who got through medical school the easy or dishonest way? Whom do we find ourselves respecting—those who are honest, responsible, dependable and consistent or those who attempt to make most or many of their interpersonal and intra-personal transactions profitable ones based on **minimal effort** or even a **misrepresentation?**

You will find that many people either acknowledge that their primary experience is one of respecting honesty, responsibility and consistency while NOT living that way with others, or they actually deny to themselves and others that they value these attributes although, usually not very convincingly.

Do you think it is possible to not fully know yourself and not be aware of this fact? WHAT IF? that **EMPTY SPOT** that you so artfully avoid internally is a result *not* of missing external attachments, social approval, or having "enough" things or activities, but of the elements of your own spirit? Do you think that it is possible to be depressed without actually being in touch with it? For those of you who ARE aware of depression, is it possible that there is even MORE sadness to your global present and/or past reality than you have been able to acknowledge or honor? WHAT IF? a good day is NOT a day you feel good but a day you FEEL! **What If? depression and anxiety are the emotional experiences resulting from the incomplete awareness of and access to one's full set of thoughts and feelings currently and historically?**

As you proceed with your self-study, these questions will arise again and THE ANSWERS WILL COME FROM THE ONLY SOURCE YOU WILL LEARN YOU CAN TRUST— YOUR OWN EXPERIENCE. Wouldn't it be interesting if you were to discover that easy in-the-moment is actually not only NOT easy at all, but that the price you are paying has hidden costs, such as the loss of yourself, which you may NOT be willing to pay as you "read YOUR fine print?" *Can you imagine* how you would experience a friendship with some-

◆

What if?

you are

unsafe and

unaware

of it

◆

one whom you have known and had contact with 24 hours a day, 7 days a week, for your entire life to date *if that individual did not consider your thoughts, feelings, and opinions important enough to honor or value*—especially if those thoughts, feelings, or opinions were different from those the "friend" wanted you to have? Is it possible that you have treated yourself this way for decades or most of your life and your response to this internal disrespect is indeed RAGE? Do you still say there is NO relationship between your in-the-moment choice of 'easy' in avoiding dealing with whatever your inner TRUTH is concerning your feelings and thoughts and your sense of emptiness, lack of self-esteem, self-respect, diminished mood, depression, social isolation and avoidance of true intimacy? Consider your fear of and resistance to change, your reduced energy and poor concentration, your poor frustration tolerance, your difficulty being alone or standing "up" for what you think/believe and, yes, even your sense that you CAN'T make it without others, booze, sex, gambling, drugs, frequent doctor visits, or perpetual connectivity with something—anything—including never-ending reassurance?

Hang in there! It does get better. However, don't forget the answers are NOT going to come from "understanding" the ideas in this reference. They are going to come from YOU and YOUR exploring what happens only **WHEN AND AS** you begin to reverse the age-old process of ignoring your own feelings and thoughts in favor of whatever distraction you have been good at generating. You WILL hear some of these sentences again at appropriate times along the way. You will also find that these ideas will evolve with additional significance as you explore the fullness of your entire discovery.

As we have previously discussed (Chapter 4), learning is a

core foundation for success. We would benefit from exploring the nature of students who confuse "being unable" to learn a task, subject or skill with the "inability" to do so. In my experience the prime block in learning lies in the student's ability and willingness to simply address and attend to the subject at hand. The issues of motivation, perseverance, effort, capacity to manage frustration, and diligence are central to the course of any successful learning endeavor and are by far, the most common barriers to learning. It becomes much more "socially acceptable" for a student to have a "learning disability" or even be "unable" to learn **in his mind** than to openly approach the issues of effort and responsibility and directly challenge his ability to succeed. This doesn't refute the existence of barriers to successful learning other than motivation, effort, persistence and diligence, however it is a common reality that literally, "where there is a will, there is a way!" We would benefit from considering whether these internal awareness and motivation issues have been dealt with fully before concluding the student is "unable" or "learning impaired." It is amazing how many parents, out of frustration with their child's resistance to learning or making her best effort, will begin to accept the child's passive offering of "I can't" and allow the child to continue on with an eventual internalization of the "explanation" of the absence of learning success as a part of her identity being an "inability." In this case, the avoidance has become experientially an "I can't." What surprises we have for these individuals when they "find us" and themselves.

One of the most basic elements of learning is simply that which is entailed by the mere attending to the subject—FOCUSING. It is directing the mind's attention to the subject at hand. Conversely, successful learning is also the process of eliminating distractions to the pursuit of addressing the subject. You will find focusing is much easier than the elimination of distractions and is a cornerstone of your future success—a fact that struggling students do not understand and successful students usually learn very early. Without FOCUS the joining of the new information with the new student's mind cannot happen.

The many distractions that living offers up in concert with our basic nature to avoid unpleasant or effort laden tasks combine to make the achievement of personal well-being and contentment at least initially, improbable, or even impossible! A wise man once said the improbable takes a long time and the impossible—just a bit longer to achieve.

An additional concept elemental in the exploration of the learning process is that of avoidance. This element is a kind of **internal active distraction.** The individual exerts either conscious and/or unconscious effort in the sidestepping of any or all of the basic steps required in learning (focus, motivation, perseverance, diligence, accessibility, and effort.) It is clear that if a would-be student for ANY reason chooses ultimately to sidestep any of the basic elements required in learning a new skill or task, that the process will be, at best, incomplete. You will see how avoidance plays a most central role in preventing individuals from becoming aware and learning about anything. Perhaps the most devastating loss is that of not understanding the simplicity of the learning process itself.

The science of physics teaches us that movement in any direction entails an understanding of direction and energy. It is precisely the "energy" component that the entity of Resistance—Stubbornness constitutes. Resistance or Stubbornness are often seen as "weaknesses" and commonly occur in the repertoire of students who consider themselves "inferior" or unsuccessful. I continue to be impressed by the individual who presents himself as "unable" or even helpless while simultaneously exerting unbelievable amounts of energy in **preventing** themselves from experiencing change in some arena of his life. You will discover that if you have the personality capability of stubbornness, then you have in essence the capacity to persevere and persist!

The issue is the direction of the effort. If one persists in the study of aeronautical engineering long enough, the outcome of becoming an astronaut is reasonable and even likely. In this case, the use of energy and effort with persistence is directed in a metaphoric "forward" direction, and we label the trait as "perseverance." If, however, the student exerts the energy in a resistance direction for ANY reason, then the "forward" direction of learning does not occur, and we call the trait "stubbornness" or "resistance" or, in its internalized final form, it may be simply experienced as "inability to perform." The consequences and outcomes of these very similar, if not equivalent, human capacities are self-explanatory and predictable.

I remember the daily experience of medical school. It was ever-challenging and the temptation to consider or worry about the eventual outcome—FAILURE or SUCCESS—was ever present. I recall an innate sense that energy spent in this manner was not only inherently exquisitely taxing but of little or no assistance in the learning process, having perhaps even a negative impact. Day by day, I continued. It seemed easier to manage some days by the hour. I granted myself a full 7-8 hours of rest religiously every night, and one day, I literally found myself in cap and gown walking down the sidewalk to graduation on the Emory University Quadrangle.

As I walked down the graduation line, I will have to admit that as I recalled the ongoing dread of the ever-present sub-liminal fear of potential failure and ridicule which assuredly would come if I didn't "graduate," there was a bit of the sur-realistic surrounding me. It was as if I had omitted the worst part of the process by simply focusing on the task at hand. God knows that stubbornness is not inherently a positive or negative force until one knows the direction of the force expended. In all my years of clinical practice, I find it extremely difficult to remember any truly "helpless" soul who did not have an unbelievable capacity to exert "resis-tance" to change! I have never felt fully comfortable accept-ing credit for assisting the successful patient (Pilgrim) in dis-covering hidden strengths within. Each found the ability to turn stubbornness in a direction of productivity and eventu-ally, often quite rapidly, a trait that heretofore had been associated with pain, regret and little or no self-esteem turned into the passkey to a full and complete exploration of self and **all that life has to offer.**

The essence of the understanding of "distraction" begins with the consideration of what drives the vulnerability. It has been the experience of this Pilgrim that the origins of dis-traction are multifaceted. Whether a central motivation exists is critical. A student who truly does not desire to pursue the subject will, irrespective of the stated intent, have tremen-dous difficulty. Whether the stated motivation is actual and true or whether there are internal "hidden" agendas is simi-larly core. Is the "distracting" element more appealing to the student than the intended subject?

If a student does not have a truly internal personal reason for pursuing the subject, then the management of ostensibly extraneous distractions becomes extremely difficult, if not impossible, to manage, especially if the extraneous element is more appealing in-the-moment. It is indeed "in-the-moment" that true heroism is defined. One gains new information step by step in-the-moment. This process becomes significant ultimately as the literal threshold of "success" or "failure." Logically, if there is a natural **internal** "attraction" to the distraction which is the basis for resisting or avoiding focusing on the task at hand, then one will find that the magnitude of interest in the distracting element may indeed not be large. A young lad faced with spending his free time in an evening with a world history or algebra text will have minimal success if he receives a telephone call from his girlfriend inviting him to the park—unless he is "focused" on getting an "A" to enhance the likelihood of a scholarship to the Air Force Academy in pursuit of an intended career in space or aeronautical engineering. In the latter event, the telephone call may produce a degree of frustration, but will unlikely detract significantly from the young man's reasons for remaining at the text and considering a "rain check" to the invitation. In the most abstract example, the young man would not choose a significant other who did not understand the magnitude and nature of his commitment to himself and his pursuits, and she would likely be an individual who would attempt to create an invitation that would not "distract" him.

One of the simplest and most misunderstood or misused concepts is that of "honesty." For the purposes of this presentation, I will offer that honesty simply represents that which is real and true without distortion or contamination. The student will likely become aware as her self-study unfolds that the complexity of the task of defining this term becomes simpler and easier as one improves focus and deals

◆

What if?

killing

your spirit

is suicidal

◆

more effectively with distractions. In this presentation, we will attribute any thought, feeling, fact or event as being honest if indeed it occurred, happened, or is occurring or happening. As in many abstract concepts, the examination of the opposite lends light to the original subject. Honesty would then be the absence of distortion, contamination or deception. Thoughts or feelings, that are resisted, repressed, denied, or not acknowledged, for whatever reason, would be handled in a dishonest fashion. The recognition of the socially negative connotation of being perceived as a "liar" or dishonest person may have become more important in our culture than the original entity itself. We are actually introducing the idea that Jack Webb repeatedly espoused, "Just the facts, Ma'am!" We are identifying the basic principle of scientific research. Let the facts lead us to the TRUTH. You WILL find with pursuit of your study that just as in science and medicine, the adherence to what is real, what is true, and what is fact will lead you and us to our source and an enhanced awareness that will allow a more complete use and appreciation of the offering and understanding of ourselves and our world.

One of the concepts found in the successful student's repertoire is the ability to honestly follow the instructions of the teacher. When a student seeks to achieve an understanding of something new, it is essential that she cooperate and follow the guidelines and recommendations of the instructor. This element becomes a primary variable on the occasion of the student's fear or resistance or distraction from the intended goal. Whether the student is pursuing the "lessons" as recommended is one of the ongoing components that the student needs to monitor. One of the most common bases for failure in a directed activity is the leaving out of a step or the distortion or modification of an exercise. The new student is STRONGLY encouraged to monitor whether she is cooperating with the presentation as suggested.

Last but certainly not least, let us examine a profoundly simple concept that continues to elude all ages—that of an individual's "Safety." For the purposes of this presentation let's assume that "Safety" or "being Safe" is the condition or circumstances pertaining to the successful biological and emotional function, survival and development of a person. In simple terms, it is the awareness of one's self in time, space and environmental circumstances physically and emotionally that allows the individual to make adaptations in favor of survival, development and creative change in the best interest of the individual. Metaphorically, if one were driving down an interstate highway, how much time would be acceptable for the driver to allow himself to be distracted from the central elements of speed, direction, and immediate environmental circumstances? You may find it hard to believe that over 90% of first time responders to this question irrespective of age answer some length of time from a few milliseconds to a few seconds. It is extremely unusual for a responder to answer Zero without oftentimes lengthy conversation and/or an attempt to "negotiate" some length of time other than zero that would be acceptable with concurrent maintenance of "safety." Nonetheless, as we are all aware, if you are going to be killed in a motor vehicle accident, statistically you will be killed most likely within 25 miles of your home; the cause of the accident will most commonly be an "insignificant" distraction to the driver (say the reaching for a comb, wallet, pencil or radio dial). As you proceed with your personal journey you will become more and more aware of how the principles of physical safety also apply to emotional safety—namely the personal awareness of one's self in all respects. In essence, we are proposing that an individual who does not know who she is, where she is, and what direction and speed she is metaphorically going is UNSAFE. You will find that this principle is painfully true of all ages.

Eleventh Assignment

PLEASE COMPLETE:

Exercise Nine, Personal "Dishonest" List, Page 204

Exercise Ten, Personal "Unsafe" List, Page 206

Make a list of all "dishonest" elements (memories, experiences, relationships, past/present endeavors) in your past and present experiences, relationships, etc. (See Figure 6, page 121.)

FIGURE SIX

DISHONEST LIST

Be specific with events, dates, people and circumstances—
NOT GENERAL—It IS laborious but will prove VERY productive.

Possible examples:

*Relationship/Partner infidelity—two affairs, first marriage, ages
31-35.*

*Manipulation of others—borrowed money from parent without
intent to repay, age 30.*

*Stealing (anything, anytime)—took $50 from Father's wallet
without permission, age 15.*

*Lying—told my junior high school English teacher I "lost" my
essay on "My Life" when I did not write it.*

*Cheating—used a "crib" sheet during a Physics final exam in
college.*

Your List:

_____   _____

_____   _____

_____   _____

_____   _____

_____   _____

Make a list of all of those choices you have made that have been against the rules, or uncooperative or unsafe. (See Figure 7, below)

FIGURE SEVEN
UNSAFE LIST

Be specific with dates, times, people—NOT GENERAL—it IS laborious but VERY productive.

Possible examples:

Driving under the influence (whether "caught" or not)—too many times to count, age 17-30.

Unprotected Sex, Multiple partners—too many times to count, age 17-40.

Speeding or reckless driving—too many times to count, age 15-50.

Being unaware of my own feelings/thoughts in deference to others, too many times to count, age 5-50 (currently).

Your List:

_____	_____
_____	_____
_____	_____
_____	_____
_____	_____

Ask yourself if you had made other choices concerning the above "dishonest/uncooperative" list items, would or could you have benefitted from doing this differently in any way?

EXAMPLES: DISHONEST (TO YOU/OTHERS): marital infidelity, unprotected sex, cheating at school, DUI, lying, stealing, using less than your full effort in any endeavor—school, athletics, music, etc., any manipulation.

UNCOOPERATIVE: speeding, illicit drug use, trying to get by with the least effort, postponing or refusing assigned tasks by an appropriately constituted authority figure.

Expect to take some time, perhaps days to weeks, to complete these lists. It may be painful, but it is essential to be as comprehensive as possible. **Leave the lists "open"** as you will find they will grow as memories return. Ask yourself whether you did/do respect these choices. As you made these choices were you fully focused on what you were choosing and what you were thinking, or were you mostly just making the choices "without thinking"—before or after —unless, of course, you were caught by some supervising/observing authority? Ask yourself if you were indeed to any extent unfocused on yourself in any manner as you made these choices. Were you in any manner "unaware" of the actual picture? Could one say you were "distracted" from what was actually happening (much like driving a car?) Would it be fair to say that to the extent you were in any fashion out of touch with yourself or your thoughts and/or feelings as they actually were—regardless of why—that you were truly "unsafe?"

Now make a list of all of the ways and times you have been and are unsafe as defined by being out of touch with the complete nature, substance or quality of your feelings, thoughts, or overall circumstance.

MAKE A COMMITMENT TO YOURSELF—You are about to meet someone you do not know or at least do not know very well and, in order to do this, you will have to be purposeful, focused, dedicated, tolerant of problems, conflicts and discomfort. **Would you expect to be able to get to know another person well without regular contact or unrestricted access to what you would let them share with you?** Generally, when getting to know another person fully and completely, the rule is that one does not limit what one shares and one is available regularly to attend to who the new person is, allowing the new person to be who he is without restraint, at least in thought and feeling. The more often you "spend attention" on this new person/relationship, the more rapidly you will get to know him. It will take time and energy—relationships are not free or easy! But, most people agree they eventually are thoroughly worth it!

YOU ARE HERE! **Simply begin and continue** with the DAILY self-awareness exercises in the **JOURNAL** (reflection and recording separately, successively) *WITHOUT reviewing what you are writing.* The initial temptation to review is great but your focus now must be to **develop the "habit" of both focusing on yourself and recording the journey.** Not only individuals but history itself agree that human experience that is not written is lost to all. This is one of the simplest AND most complex parts of the journey. Do not let ANYTHING prevent you from pursuing the simple ideas of paying attention regularly to what your thoughts and feelings are daily and RECORDING them.

From time to time, perhaps even regularly, (for some people this next phase can last as long as they ALLOW it) you will find it inconvenient, disagreeable, or even at times emotionally and/or physically painful to proceed. You will discover that avoidance, denial, ignoring the issues, and disregard for yourself will feel eminently easier IN-THE-MOMENT, and you will become distracted by events that occur naturally in your life (some of which may even be disasters and tragedies.) The distraction, resistance, and avoidance are natural components of the process and do not indicate Failure or Defeat!

Just PAY ATTENTION TO WHEN YOU GET DISTRACTED — be sure to journal about this as well, and note how things go for you during these times. How would you describe your attention, mood quality and stability, concentration, sense of well-being, motivation, energy, endurance, and overall pleasure levels when you are distracted? Once you have traversed this experience you have a choice to QUIT and return to the "wonderfully" successful and "easier" former lifestyle OR continue with your self-study. Here is where the outcome is defined by your perseverance. You have the opportunity to CONVERT that previously discussed STUBBORNNESS into a potential asset whose value at this point you are unable to fully evaluate.

Continue and complete your "dishonest" and "unsafe" lists. As you do this you will note that the getting back on track is a little less mysterious; however, depending on how unfocused (distracted) you have allowed yourself to get and how long you have "been away" from yourself, the "rediscovery" process may take enormous energy. Don't allow yourself to be discouraged; remember, disappointment is a function of expectation and is in itself a distraction. This process is indeed part of the learning and is not defeat. Once refocused, you are now a SUCCESS even though you don't FEEL that way. The process still does not feel secure, and you probably—and understandably so—do not feel you can rely on or trust it. You are beginning within yourself to allow yourself to be aware of the positive differences that are slowly beginning to surface within your awareness (concentration, mood quality and stability, evenness, motivation, energy level, intimacy.) The distraction process will occur over and over. Each time you discover you are off track, regardless of how quickly you discover it, the refocus process will be a CHOICE and EFFORT. You will learn that the sooner you discover the distraction, the easier it is to get back on track.

Twelfth Assignment

The easiest way to quickly identify this process is to sit down with a pencil and paper and make two lists. **Label one "Self" and one "Non-self"** and under each of these categories list how your monitors—mood, concentration, stability, etc.—are affected by whether you are focused or not.

Example: Non-focused/Non-self: concentration up or down, motivation—up or down, energy—up or down, etc. You may even use a 0 to +10 rating scale to designate relative changes. (See Figure 8, Page 127.)

FIGURE EIGHT

	Self-Focused	Non self-Focused
MOOD	_____	_____
CONCENTRATION	_____	_____
MOTIVATION	_____	_____
ENERGY	_____	_____
SELF ESTEEM	_____	_____
CREATIVITY	_____	_____
CONTENTMENT	_____	_____

You will note that even though you may not be actually aware of whether you are primarily focused on your own thoughts and feelings, you are generally aware of your mood, concentration, motivation, energy, etc. And, if indeed these variables respond to focus predictably, you will quickly be able to identify your mind set focus as soon as you become aware of the diminished concentration, mood, energy or motivation that every Pilgrim describes.

At this point you have become a TRAVELER. It would appear that continued focus and self-exploration is associated with general enhancements for you in any way? There is indeed a relationship between awareness, focus, and responsibility to the overall quality of your experience and, yes, self-respect. You are beginning to understand that doing good does not necessarily mean "feeling" good—at least until after one allows oneself to "be," as Shakespeare said. Responsibility does appear to pay in the "long run." You by now, or soon will have, experienced an episode of having ALLOWED yourself to feel some negative or painful experience without denying or avoiding it. And, SURPRISE! You are stronger than your pain! Although you felt "bad" during the actual exploration, you began to feel "good" about yourself when you were able to manage the experience itself. YOU ARE EXPERIENCING SELF-RESPECT!

What would it be like to be able to do this on an ongoing basis irrespective of the stressor or event(s)? It is a common barrier to progress for the Pilgrim to take her focus off of the road that leads to the goal and, instead, think about where she is headed; you have just been distracted and your growth has halted! Keep your eyes "ON THE ROAD" and your progress WILL continue. TIME will **slowly** become your ally and support. It is OK to register your ongoing benefits, such as, enhanced self esteem, improved mood and concentration, increased energy and motivation. Those are feelings; however, don't be distracted by "FUTURE" considerations or even current success. Keep going! It is not unlike a new driver learning how to monitor a car's speed and direction. How quickly this can change without COMPLETE TOTAL FOCUS irrespective of "why" or "how much" to turn the steering wheel to maintain direction and avoid wide swings in the car's course. The leading cause of motor vehicular death is simple loss of focus concerning the car's direction, speed, or path due to a distraction such as a radio channel selection, picking up a pen, or dialing a car phone.

CHAPTER NINE

focus vs

Distractions

Discipline
and Patience

Until I feared I would lose it, I never loved
to read. One does not love breathing.

~ Harper Lee, To Kill A Mockingbird

The capacity to direct and maintain our attention toward our own feelings and thoughts is clearly one of, if not **the**, most demanding and labor-intensive experiences in developing self-awareness. Often those challenges which we believe to be insurmountable ultimately become the most fondly remembered and impassioned experiences of life. Despite the effort involved **initially**, the magnitude of the energy required is NOT an indicator of effort required in the **future** once the basic skills are attained. This is exemplified in the energy required to learn a new language before and after the acquisition of "fluency."

As you proceed with your DAILY personal self-reflections, you will encounter many different distractions, both the anticipated external stimuli and the unforeseen "internal" ones. The successful continuation of your journey depends upon one relatively simple concept. **At any time you are aware of your thoughts and/or feelings, you become less aware of the periphery and distraction.** When you become distracted and focused on anything other than your own feelings and thoughts, you will find you are more "comfortable" in-the-moment with what you are doing out of habit alone. However, you will again become aware of being susceptible to anxiety and a lack of certainty. That ever-present sense of incompleteness, emptiness, and a desire to acquire external approval or acceptance will creep up on you. You are reentering what your fellow travelers refer to as "the hole." Your mood will become more changeable and determined by external events, and you will immediately attempt to control your environment—usually with a sense that "you've lost it"—of course we are referring to YOUR SELF!

Thirteenth Assignment

PLEASE COMPLETE:

Exercise Thirteen, Personal "Distractions" List, Page 211

Initially, you will find that just being aware of yourself will take great discipline and effort. You will discover that even the successes you have experienced to date will not in and of themselves be enough to sustain you in maintaining your continued self-awareness. There will be intrusive thoughts of how you "should" be or what you "ought" to be thinking or feeling. You will repeatedly question the acceptability of your own experience from many purviews, both internal and external. It is much like looking in the mirror and asking repeatedly, "Is that actually me?...there in the mirror?" You should expect this questioning. You may remember and recall from your existing reservoir of wisdom the pattern you know so well of how it goes when you meet another person and go through the "getting to know you" sequence. How many times in an intense relationship that encompasses much contact time and significant accessibility does one question both herself and the "new" attachment (person) from many perspectives—such as credibility, dependability, endurance, etc.?

At times, you may experience intense anxiety related to change. This aspect of the new student has been described by many as akin to the experience of the "newlywed" or the young child attempting to ride his first "two-wheeler." The general sensation of having just let go of what is known, solid or stable, as defined by the "old way," namely security from the "outside"—others' opinions or approval—can be immense. **Don't be surprised if you falter more than once and with much intensity in the doing! It truly is an essential, genuine part of the learning process—NOT an indication of failure or an inability to achieve your goal!**

You will have a sense of a loss of balance after you have allowed yourself to maintain your new self-awareness for even brief periods. This is to be expected and is a sign of further progress. As a completely new traveler, you may experience the initial attempts in focusing on yourself as confusing, difficult to achieve, or perhaps, even "impossible" or unreal. You may experience intense hesitation and reluctance even after your initial awareness that when you are successfully focusing on yourself, the result is always productive and sustaining! Don't despair. Your first attempts on the "two-wheeler" are fraught with spills and abrasions. Eventually, successful bike riders become "based" in the connection that occurs for them with the initial, brief episodes of balance which transpire when the rider pushes

What if?

the easy

way isn't

easy at all

◆

What if?

you can

create

time

◆

on the pedals and moves forward. The rider gains the ability to steer without worry or fear of injury or falling. Success becomes an experience of achievement, not a management of fear or pain, although the initial phase of this learning certainly may have been experienced as primarily painful. The traveler then amasses enough sequential learning to establish a foundation of achievement. The positive nature of the overall process outweighs the management of pain or loss. The "good" stuff is worth going through the "bad" stuff.

Do you remember that the fear of the fall when learning to ride your bike was greater than the actual injury itself? You will also want to recall that, as with the bicycle, the feared event, "forward motion," is actually that which defines the **stability** of the bicycle and the **ability** of the rider **to steer!** Similarly, you will eventually find and experience that self-focus—that which you initially found or felt to be so cumbersome or even impossible is now "forward motion." Allowing one's own experience to be primary or central ABOVE ALL OTHER CONSIDERATIONS including discomfort or emotional pain is the impetus behind the push of the pedal. You will not believe me or your fellow travelers until you have "pushed your own pedals" and allowed "your bicycle" to move forward—allowing yourself to license your own experience as primary and irrefutable. These periods will gradually lengthen over time and with practice. You will not actually fully understand (until after you allow it to happen a few times) why you seem to return to the "old way" despite the inefficiency and lack of success you experience using the more familiar method.

Wonderful things begin to emerge as you find your own private, personal courage to listen to, attend to, concentrate on and, yes, even begin to register an internal sense of "reverence" concerning your own voice in an unencumbered fashion with no distortion, no distraction, inhibition, disrespect, modification, rejection, denial, or denigration. A quieting occurs. You become aware of a marked disinterest in things previously held as essential to pleasure or survival (e.g., various external stimuli, constant distractions, "antiboredom" devices or relationships.) You begin to experience any disruptions or intrusions into your own private space much as the prayerful monk would experience the noisy entry of a group of partying adolescents bursting into a deeply religious ceremony or sacrament. You are truly experiencing your own "Holy Place," and along with the nature and simplicity of this experience comes a general sense of contentment and solidarity. You also experience a sense of tolerance of others and patience with those who, as of yet, do not understand. In place of irritation and resentment previously experienced with these people, you develop a desire to teach, support, be patient with and instruct. Your enemies become your friends, and hatred, envy, competition and jealousy are naturally transformed into fraternity, brotherhood, humanity and the collective worship of the opportunity of life itself.

You learn how to let your own full complete spirit "breathe" not only in an unrestricted, unencumbered manner, but beyond, to a position of honor and sacred reverence. This ability naturally and effortlessly translates to others and all of life itself. You have indeed recreated time and memory as well as lengthened your life by adding awareness and personal meaning. You have subtracted loss of awareness and defined yourself as greater than the stresses and pain brought to you historically and currently. You have gained access to all that you are and may become. You now

♦

What if? freedom and creativity are found in self-focus

♦

truly know what is meant by knowing your own strength—knowing yourself. The next great challenge is for you to become a teacher.

Fellow Pilgrims describe their experiences initially and subsequently as follows:

"I guess, I still haven't made that commitment to myself...I still tend to think if I put things off they will happen...I'll end up doing it some time...I'm not getting it through my thick skull...I'm still resisting...I'm still unsafe...yes, I am very stubborn...I still think...or want others to be able to do it for me...I want the people around me to be supportive and make me work...but I have to do it for myself...I know without a commitment to myself...the distractions will be impossible...I need a personal commitment...it will still be hard, painful...it's like my needs are fighting my wants...I'm just not dealing with the urgency or the emergency...I really...don't want to put my survival in anyone else's hands...I know I need to be honest with how hard this is...I'm not isolating as much...I've felt I'm causing my own problems...but I can't help it...I made a bracelet that says "what is my truth"...it reminds me...focusing on others only works for a split second and then it's gone...I figured if I did it more it would last longer...I'm trying...no, I'm squirming...my truth now is I struggle with responsibility and try to put it on other things like I did with my bracelet...I abandon myself when it gets hard...I've despised, hated, neglected me...I don't know me...when I'm only focused on me, my lonely becomes different...my alone...it is like...a miracle inside...I guess I've known this all along...I just ignored it...the 'to be or not to be' means more to me now...."

...another Pilgrim...

*"I felt like I had a setback with my learning experience
...as things came on I was more comfortable with learning and understanding how...later I was extremely emotional and felt out of control...had to try very, very hard
not to make wrong decisions...and run off at the
mouth...I had anger, disappointment and hurt...I felt I'd
come so far...to fall in a big hole...I didn't think I'd have
trouble with this hole...thank goodness I didn't act emotionally, felt safe, relieved...like I'm stronger than the
hole...I was very afraid...and without learning...I'd have
made a total disaster...I took time, reflected, stayed alone,
and lost a good "superficial" friend...the hole created a
new step for me...every hole is like no other hole...'til you
define yourself as a pit...I wrote, thought, eventually
replaced emotions, calmed down...the more I wrote
about it, the more I understood what was happening...with me and how I would be out of control without
me...if I didn't invite myself into the hole...I wouldn't be
there...I found myself again...it's startling, frightening
and self satisfying...I thought about journaling and me
and all that has taught me...and without it I'd have been
in the hole...I know without self-respect what I have is a
nightmare...nothing...I used to say I was in the GREAT
NOTHING...I haven't been in the Nothing in a long
time...3 months is a long time to be away from
Nothing...this process is like a card catalog in a
library...a reference point...I'm lost in the library with
hundreds of books...the catalog helps me find what I
need...when I fell in the hole, I thought of...the lessons, the
wisdom...I started reading back in my journal...a whole
day of your life...is wasted...without journaling..."*

...another Pilgrim...

"Who do I have to live with?...others matter...but, I'm the one I have to put up with 24/7...why do I please others so much?...I'm more and more aware of...life without my own self-respect is not much...I always feel better when I do the right thing...I really can't fast talk Mother Nature...there really isn't any difference between driving down the interstate highway and being a person...in terms of how much or often you have to keep your eyes on your road...truth, my truth, really is what life is...nothing has worked better for me...than my own...self-respect...."

CHAPTER TEN

Experience,
The Universal
Basis of
Truth ~ Belief

Practicing To Be
and Living
the Adventure

To be, or not to be: that is the question.

– William Shakespeare, Hamlet

Just let it be, let it—you—happen. Take a walk. Visit a museum or gallery. Take a vacation to a private place. Go see a movie, attend a symphony or concert or lecture. Visit a Chapel reflectively. Write a poem about something or someone important to you. Tell a dear friend something you have been thinking about for years without regard (in the telling) to their response. Sit down and actually create the "dream home" you have always thought of having—with emphasis on the components and the characteristics, NOT the having. DO ALL OF THIS ALONE! Do not allow anything to intrude into your solitude, personal access, experience and expression. Do not allow anything to distract you from your personal experience for any reason.

Fourteenth Assignment

PLEASE COMPLETE:

Exercise Fourteen, Personal Growth Environments, Page 212

Note the difference over time in maintaining a relationship with your self and the experience itself. Remember this will take time. Your experiences ALONE are opportunities to feel and think without distraction or distortion from without. Note how even a simple thing such as a bird flying by can take you away from the initial sight itself and initiate a complete personal creativity of thought which springs from within yourself and becomes a kind of personal stage not in search of an audience. The Pilgrim may then have a spontaneous discovery of a multitude of thoughts and feelings about freedom, nature, and courage as a result of a very simple event. Note that this is a continual process and, in essence, all of life's stimuli have now become opportunities to access and express yourself. Orson Wells, the great director and screenwriter, once commented concerning watching vs writing screenplays that viewing others' creative works only spurred him to go out and write the story his own way. He could not tolerate the experience of "accepting" the original author's plot, story sequence, ending, etc. You will experience gradual improvement in your ability to allow yourself to connect with yourself without distraction, even by major issues and events, and you will begin to be able to simultaneously track your experience and the periphery without contamination of one by the other. The result is an unbelievable sense of personal freedom, solidarity and purpose, and an enhanced tolerance of previously experienced intrusions and distractions. You become more patient, mature and purposeful and more efficient in using your time. You are much less willing to use your time in pursuit of events, people or experiences which you perceive as foreign or dissonant to you.

Revel in the opportunity of getting to know another (both those who understand and do not make demands upon you **and** those who do **not** understand and constantly seek reassurance from you, attempting to settle the ever present conflict within themselves which you remember so well.) Notice how aspects of the other person's experience that before would have been disagreeable to you are now sources of learning and opportunities to explore the diversity of being human. **You have lost your need to have others be like you or agree with you.** Don't be surprised if when you truly begin to "listen" to others that the previously irritating personality traits of others may indeed become more familiar to you and even clearly be recognized by you as being just those same qualities that you have historically had the most difficulty in accepting in yourself. You are learning about the nature of conflict. **To know your "enemy" is to know yourself.**

Note the patience you now naturally have with those that are still in a panic or are in control economies. Note how you see your own journey within the junior traveler's struggle. Be aware, as you explore ways to facilitate someone's awareness from your natural inclination to share, how he sets up all types of barriers. The unwillingness to have an awareness of himself is in opposition to the stated motivation to get to know one's self. As you learn how to gently and patiently negotiate these mountain stream stepping stones, you become aware of your own learning as it grows clearer and develops more rapidly as you live your truth. To know is to demonstrate the beingness of yourself and your constant attention to learning. The new Pilgrim will reject and deny; however, if you are persistent, diligent, respectful and truthful in your patience and accessibility, not pushing or offering for any reason other than to serve as a resource,

*What if?
the
answers
are within*

*

What if?

you can

know your

own truth

and live

it daily

*

the student WILL listen and return time and time again. Upon each return, you will have a little more of the student's attention and trust as he is actually learning bit by bit to experience himself—NOT you.

You are on the way to the most rewarding aspect of your journey. Patience, focus and accessibility together with non-judgmental, well-timed assistance are your hallmarks. You must wait for freedom to continue from the Pilgrim. It will not always come in the form of open verbal statements, but may, at times, simply come by evidence of one's company alone. Certain Pilgrims will observe how you address your life in whatever ways they may be able to pick up on, and your first entreé as a resource is whether you are able "to be" or not. One cannot teach something one cannot use themselves. We will deal with this more in the **Addendum (Buyer Beware!)**

You become more of a student of everything life has to offer when learning about the human experience. You now address and strikingly note that even the youngest child spews forth great wisdom and perception quite openly and adeptly. Once again, beauty previously missed is discovered.

You become profoundly grateful for your gifts. Your new awareness is described by many as a new birth or beginning. You are also quietly aware of the loss of time prior to your awareness and the limits on time you imposed by the issue of LIFE'S longevity. Your panic in the anticipation of loss is now replaced by simple gratitude for the grace of the full enhancement of life itself. **Primary fear has ceased to have a hold on you, being spontaneously and naturally replaced by the experience of life itself—the only truly satisfying experi-**

ence available. *Satisfaction does not come from outside, from others, from stimulation or from distraction from your own personal truth.* You now know what it means to "be high" or perhaps simply... "to be." You now have some-one who is with you always, who knows the TRUTH about you, and accepts you for who you really are; someone who not only wants to spend time with you but DEMANDS it; someone who will defend your experience to all challenges at your instant beck and call and with whom the empty space within is NO MORE. You are no longer lonely, inade-quate, helpless, dependent, insecure, anxious, or UNCER-TAIN.

CHAPTER ELEVEN

The
Journey

Experience Relief,
Freedom, and
Creativity

*You cannot perceive beauty but
with a serene mind.*

- Henry David Thoreau

As you pursue your examination of yourself, you will discover many new and wonderful experiences, often in subtle ways. You are, of course, not making judgements about the quality of the feelings and thoughts as they emerge, and you are "fighting the good fight" as you face your truth. The necessity to do the work in stages may arise, especially if you "stumble" into an arena that is particularly painful, embarrassing, or perhaps even "disgraceful" to you. In this case, you simply allow yourself to do as much of the "recognition" and "attention" work as you can manage at any one time. It is not unlike having a friend present themselves to you after having received some dreadful or painful news. And, as they speak to you, you find that your own tolerance of the pain may have limits.

The natural limitation response is at least two-fold. The first is, of course, the old and well-known entity of simple avoidance, which by now, you are able to recognize and confront, albeit still with much effort. The second is the sense that if you continue to allow your friend unrestricted access to you, the total impact of your listening and accessibility may indeed create an emotional reality for you that will in and of itself define **your own** primary mood. You then, predictably, are spontaneously inclined—even driven—to withdraw or guard yourself from the contact (at least internally.) You then choose whether to let your friend know that you are feeling the need to limit your accessibility to her pain. It is this latter process that the higher level student learns to manage by learning to identify the difference between a kind of graduated, controlled accessibility to the pain versus a partial or total exclusion of the pain. You may allow yourself to experience your friend's pain completely in increments that do not distort the substance or quality of your own experience. You challenge yourself to be available in PORTIONS with your goal being to complete all of the experience presented. This may be done in emotional installments—your pace, your process. **Your** experience is where your primary focus is.

The mind is, as we know, a wondrous element that has the capacity to store, recall, portion and process experience with and without distortion. When you apply these mental tools to your own internal, (usually painful) experience (just as you would respect a friend's pain or sadness—at your own pace) the end result is not distorted. As you develop the capacity to manage the external-interpersonal-sources of sadness, you are simultaneously developing the capacity to manage your own internal sadness. It is much like reading a long and complex book. You can read a line, paragraph, page or chapter a day without editing, deleting, or skipping sections and limit the immediate impact of the entire work without cheating yourself of the full value of the complete offering. One can move a huge mound of soil with tweezers, a teaspoon, shovel, or backhoe every second, minute or hour regularly or irregularly. It is the regular and diligent approach that is most closely associated with the highest quality learning.

You are finding that as you allow yourself to process and experience ALL of your current and past experiences you are indeed, in a sense, shoveling a large amount of coal. As you do so, with each spoonful, shovel full, or even dump truck full, the mound gets smaller, despite the reality that each day brings "new" coal for your mound—some days in different amounts and density. You become literally stronger and more adept in the shoveling process with progressively less resistance and anxiety as you face each new event or circumstance.

Your vision is slowly clearing. You are calmer, and you find that approaching moment-by-moment the challenge of identifying YOUR perspective and intent is becoming easier and more satisfying irrespective of the complexity and magnitude of the challenge. You are experiencing yourself as more "together", more complete, less encumbered, and free. Some even describe a sense of enhanced awareness of life itself. Time is becoming more precious to you and "objects" (things other than your experience) progressively less so. A general sense of release and relief is readily a part of your ongoing experience. You are literally coming out of the fog. **After allowing yourself to feel, integration begins. You begin to feel the release.**

At this time, you may compare your experience now with how things were in the beginning. You may choose to re-read early entries in your journal. It is recommended that this be done only for limited periods of time because you can become distracted from your **current** experience by the reflective process. You are traveling across a long roadway,

•

What if?

a good

day is not

a day you

feel good,

but simply

a day that

you feel

•

and it is acceptable from time to time to think about the entire trip to date; however, not so as to slow or halt the current or **ongoing** aspects of your progress which must be maintained in order to continue the primary growth process. It is a time for reflection and comparison—perhaps even a bit of personal gratitude toward YOURSELF for having taken those early fragile UNCERTAIN steps of choosing to get to know yourself completely. It is always acceptable to thank a good friend for something they have given you that makes your life more meaningful and rewarding. **Take a well deserved (brief) pat on the back and continue on.**

You are becoming aware, initially, only on occasion and then, in a striking, yet subtle manner, more often and with less effort. Your fear of losing the new awareness dissipates slowly as you continue to pursue your endeavor. You are becoming conscious of the magnitude and vastness of the experiences your mind and spirit comprehend moment-to-moment which you have either missed altogether along the way or have only briefly noted and lost (at least until this rebirth experience.) Your clarity increases only with persistent pursuit. You are more aware of everything and the experience of humility and reverence permeates you as you become immersed in the complete wonder of life in its fullest. Words like unbelievable, beautiful, complete, holy, grace, exciting, exhilarating, peace, wonder and patient begin to naturally emerge from within your depths. You begin to have thoughts of all the people you know and care about, and you now understand their struggle more completely as you do your own. You now understand the prior natural reluctance to define yourself in terms of places, people, possessions, or even ideas. **You are becoming one with your time and spirit.** You are amazed and perhaps even a lit-

tle embarrassed at the simplicity of what you have discovered. You find yourself drawn to quiet, natural and reflective
places. You have become more aware of the incredible number of distractions from your newness of life than you had
realized even during the beginning weeks of your first learning. **You automatically know that all that you are is all that
there is, and this is quietly enough.**

The word **real** now has meaning never before fully experienced. This new information is available to anyone who
will allow themselves **to be.** You quietly chuckle to yourself
and know that you will no longer want. You desire to share
what you have and are simultaneously drawn to expression
and exploration of your own fullness. You now understand
the basis for those old feelings and thoughts like guilt, envy,
should, ought, revenge, and bitterness. These feelings of
inadequacy simply and naturally, without effort, disappear
from your world. You have a striking new openness and
peace about you. Simplicity and gratitude permeate your
entire spirit, and you recognize that all creatures of nature
are universal gifts. **Life has become beautiful and you have
become Life.** No longer is a good day a day that you feel
good. A good day has become simply a day, a day that
you—feel.

It is now time to reflect on the nature, course, direction,
quality and extent of the journey which you are about. I am
sure by this time you have already done so, at least in small
increments or when those around you have made observations about dramatic changes in the way you operate or
relate to your world. These changes may literally have been
outside of your awareness prior to having the changes
brought to your attention.

The well-focused student can indeed lose track of the relative ground covered over the course during the process. The awakening can be both the consciously perceived elements of the daily work and self-appraisal, as well as the silent shifts. These WILL be called to your attention by others as you exhibit these changes in a manner that is perceived by others to be sustained and significant. People will begin telling you that they see you as different, calm, grounded, and more centered. You will notice that at times, previously high anxiety or intensity has either significantly diminished or abated entirely. You may even experience a kind of quiet concern for the absence of this previously ever-present "signal anxiety" that you heretofore used as a kind of emotional sentinel. You may wonder if you are as "safe" as you feel. Are you just missing the possible threats in your life? You will later learn as you go that it is possible to reintegrate your peripheral awareness as a necessary part of your immediate survival and that this process is much easier, smoother and less energy-consuming than before. It is still important to "look both ways" literally and metaphorically before you "cross the street." It is a matter of fact that fellow travelers, be they participants in the exploration of their own truth or not, WILL make note of changes in you. If you are perceived as genuine, maintained, and productive, and having truly challenged your own avoidance of truth, you will stimulate others interest in their own journey. They will often challenge you with great energy—even negatively at times, literally "testing" the solidarity of your focus. It is nearly magical that the testing of your achievement will be the challenger's denial and need to validate that there is no way you could be willing to have your own experience truly independent of the observer's approval.

• • •

The next exercise (Exercise 11) should NOT be completed until the student has logged a minimum of three months of regular daily journaling and is CLEAR about the experience of "being FOCUSED" and experientially familiar with what it feels like to "be DISTRACTED." DO NOT COMPLETE THIS SECTION UNTIL YOU HAVE DONE SO AS DIRECTED. You may journey forward to Chapter 12 if you are not quite ready for this experience.

When you are ready, go back to the initial list of the undesirable traits you had in the beginning, to your "dishonest/unsafe" lists, and note the categories of issues you identified as unpleasant or problematic—such as, concentration, mood, self-esteem, self-respect, motivation, energy, intimacy, perseverance, achievement, contentment, etc. Again, please rate yourself in each of these categories in terms of what happens to each of these elements when you are and are not focused on your own vs others' or peripheral experiences. (See Figure 9, page 156) (See also Exercise number Eleven, Page 207)

Fifteenth Assignment

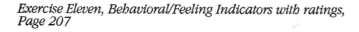

PLEASE NOW COMPLETE:

Exercise Eleven, Behavioral/Feeling Indicators with ratings, Page 207

(Subjective Qualitative Experiential Rating Scale) SQERS

FIGURE NINE

Suggested Categories:	Initial Rating (-10 to +10)	Focused Rating (-10 to +10)
Concentration	_____	_____
Mood	_____	_____
Self-Esteem	_____	_____
Self-Respect	_____	_____
Motivation	_____	_____
Energy	_____	_____
Depression	_____	_____
Anxiety	_____	_____
Intimacy	_____	_____
Perseverance	_____	_____
Achievement	_____	_____
Contentment	_____	_____
Others:		
_____	_____	_____
_____	_____	_____
_____	_____	_____
_____	_____	_____
_____	_____	_____
_____	_____	_____

Do you see the difference? Is that difference predictable? In other words, when you ARE focused on your own feelings and thoughts WITHOUT distraction, does the same impact on the above variables occur? For example, when you are focused on yourself, do you find that your concentration and mood are ALWAYS improved? When you lose your FOCUS, do you lose your concentration and mood?

If this is the case, then one can logically conclude that whatever elements in your life support and enhance your ability and expertise in maintaining your focus on your feelings and thoughts (as a central process NEVER to be given up) will also allow you to maintain an improved mood and increased concentration. Namely, all of those elements that you were initially displeased with are decreased or even eliminated with the emergence of your focus. You now understand what it means to have access to and "control" over your experience. Isn't it interesting how most students agree that the beginner's fantasy or expectation of how it will be when he masters a task is never actually predictive of the literal outcome? Often, it is profoundly different. So much so, that the student has a hard time going back in his mind and accepting that he may have been so naive as to have imagined that the endpoint could have been so simplistically defined. An example would be what an attorney, clergyman, surgeon, or musical virtuoso might retrospectively say about their initial vs ultimate experiences of having anticipated what it would be like to achieve their professional goal vs what life actually consisted of after they experienced themselves as having achieved their goal.

In this respect, most Pilgrims indicate that the actual experience of being an independent, self-reliant individual is nothing like they had anticipated—for what they were initially hoping for was actually a part of the barrier keeping them from achieving the Goal! Namely, there was an expectation that being a fully functioning individual would be easy, free of pain, free of conflict, free of sorrow and without significant losses. The actual outcome is entirely different, and most, if not all, agree it is more real, rewarding, and pervasively creative than anything that could have been imagined! Indeed, it IS better and yes, EASIER! It is just not in the manner initially envisioned by the novice. **You see, expectation in and of itself is one of the distractions; and in and of itself, expectation is not "real"—it is, in fact, a futuristic distraction from the "real stuff."**

One useful technique in assessing the nature and magnitude of your emerging change has been successfully employed by those that have gone before you. TRY THIS. Go back to the mind set you were in originally—before you began your journey. It may help to again pick up your **discontented list** and **review** it. This will probably bring back the qualitative experiences you were having when you chose to pursue your current direction of self-study. Remember that your inclination to avoid those feelings IS predictable, "normal" AND something you can address, experience and successfully negotiate. All successful students acknowledge reluctance to address the learning in some form during the course of their learning endeavor. It is the handling of the reluctance or resistance to the learning that discriminates between success and failure.

FORGE AHEAD. Are you surprised that it is taking effort to bring that initial experience fully back to you? You were convinced that the very same constellation of experiences would "always" be your primary experience and would be "unchangeable." Is it hard to remember "just how bad it really was?" **For your own benefit, don't EVER forget what it was like!** Those who do not understand history ARE compelled to repeat it. One of the most common "relapse" issues is the "forgetting" of HOW BAD, BAD WAS. In order to support, enhance, and define the importance of the subjective changes that are happening, please recall the OVERALL general sense of discontent, pain, isolation, uncertainty, and/or fear that permeated your life. Imagine a numeric spectrum that, for the sake of comparison, goes from minus 10 (-10) on the left to a midpoint of 0 to a top end point of plus 10 (+10) where -10 represents the point at which an individual "gives up" and is literally self-destructive (e.g., attempts suicide), 0 represents a kind of numbness or emotionally neutral place where no feeling is experienced, and on to +10, the highest quality of experience you can imagine ever having (e.g., complete independence, contentment, spontaneous unencumbered creativity and unbridled courage). (See Figure 10.)

FIGURE TEN

Subjective Qualitative Experiential Rating Scale (SQERS)

Death	Despair	Numb	Pleased	Contentment
-10_____	-5 _____	0 _____	+5 _____	+10
	A		B	

Give yourself two numeric ratings. The first (A) is a rating that you would have given yourself at the beginning in terms of how you generally felt day-to-day **before** beginning this process. The second (B) is the rating you today would retrospectively give yourself at the start after having begun this process. Have you given yourself a lower rating now than you would have at the time of the outset of your self-study? If so, you are among the vast majority of travelers. It seems that the more we discover of ourselves, the more completely and thoroughly we are able to assess where we are at any one point in time. Most people who are not fully aware of themselves are initially not fully aware of the magnitude and quality of their despair until they begin to directly explore their side-stepped depths.

Now rate the overall quality of life experience that you would have given at that initial time and the rating you would now give to assess the initial experience. Please also give yourself a current rating.

Concurrently, look back at your unsafe/dishonest lists and rate yourself in terms of what percentage of your total personal truth you think you had access to in the beginning. Don't forget to give yourself a rating now that you would have given at the time you started, as well as a current rating of what percentage of your personal total truth you now have access to. Have the numbers changed? Has your percentage of personal truth increased as you have pursued your self-study and exploration? Do you think there is an association between the increased personal truth percentage and the (assumed) increase in the overall quality of life? Most, if not all, Pilgrims at this stage emphatically agree that the enhancement in their overall life experience is directly related to the nature, quality and extent of the honesty, as well as the consistency of their ability to maintain personal focus upon their own internal experience or truth. Pilgrims agree this understanding is a heart awakening. **Indeed, the quality of personal awareness or honesty with one's self appears to be directly related to the experienced quality of life itself.** Who would ever have thought that the quality of a person's honesty with himself and his ability to maintain this reality is **one** if not **the** central determining factor concerning the overall quality of life? Indeed, taking the easy or dishonest way out (with yourself or others) is in fact not easy at all.

At this point, it is not unusual for the new student to rank herself as having moved from an initial (A) -5 or -10 to a subsequent (B) +3 or +5, with a respective increase of personal "truth" from an initial 1-2% to say 30-70%. (See/Use Figure 11.)

FIGURE ELEVEN

Initial New Student SQERS

Death	Despair	Numb	Pleased	Contentment
-10_____	-5 _____	0 _____	+5 _____	+10
	A		B	

If these numbers are even close to being accurate, then the individual who has gone minimally from (A) a -5 to (B) a +5 by increasing her personal honesty from 1-2% to minimally 30% (by our example) has experienced a 200% improvement with approximately 30% or 1/3 full effort! (See/Use Figure 12.)

FIGURE TWELVE

Current New Student SQERS

Death	Despair	Numb	Pleased	Contentment
-10_____	-5 _____	0 _____	+5 _____	+10
	A		B	

Not a bad return on any investment. Most students at this point are grinning a bit sheepishly—astonished, unbelieving and eager as they consider: "WHAT IF? using my numbers (which I think you will see and agree in time are a GROSS UNDERESTIMATE of the potential) is not an accurate representation of the expected resulting experience I will feel if I increase my 30% effort to 90+% or more?" (See/Use Figure 13)

FIGURE THIRTEEN

Student's Anticipated SQERS Potential

Death   Despair   Numb   Pleased   Contentment
-10_____ -5 _____ 0 _____ +5 _____ +10......+?
              A   B

The individual could indeed experience (if maintaining without distraction a focus and concentration on ALL of his personal truth ALL of the time) an even and relatively unfaltering enhancement of a magnitude of 600% of the initial beginning level of functioning and quality of life! As you have anticipated, the punch line has yet to emerge. WHAT IF? your actual personal truth increase has been less than 10% or even less than 2% with the above referenced enhancement? (See Figure 14.)

FIGURE FOURTEEN

Author's Statement of SQERS Potential

Death   Despair   Numb   Pleased   Contentment
-10_____ -5 _____ 0 _____ +5 _____ +10..........+?
              A   B

That would put the ballpark increase in the total quality of life achievable by you in the ranking of 10 to 50 times the improvement experienced to date! Most students at this point have much difficulty even imagining life at that level; even individuals who have spent significant parts of their lives "high" or intoxicated physically struggle with the vision of what it would be like to be in a place such as we are discussing in a predictable and dependable way on a maintained, even keel without peripheral support or chemicals. These individuals then (in a most awestruck fashion) agree that even they have "never been HIGH!"

Those who have gone before you describe the subjective appraisal of their growth in the following manner:

"I'm losing the "less" from the hopeless...it's coming from me...how I feel depends on whether I'm doing it...if I'm doing it...I feel great...when I don't, I feel like crap...when I focus on my distractions, I don't do it...there is still a part of me that says I don't need to do it...I'm stubborn...to think I can do things my way...my first distraction is me...I tell myself I can get by...I'm the one who makes these distractions...it's never worked for me...when I came in I was close to killing myself...a -10 or a -9 ...I'm a 0 now overall...some positive and some negative...it's the focus that's made it happen...I've only shared 75%, no, probably only 50% of my truth...there is a relationship between honesty, responsibility and freedom...there were things on my mind I wasn't thinking of that affected how I felt...I guess it's possible that I've shared even less...it's good that there is more to me...maybe 10-50 times as much...if I continue...I believe that I am my only enemy...I can handle being wet...the rain...my fear...."

...another Pilgrim...

"I really know I don't respect manipulation and avoiding responsibility...I still find myself hoping that will change and the "easy" way will work...but it doesn't...I realize I'm alone whether I like it or not...and I need to be all that I am or go back to the old way...I know being real is a lot better...when I came in I was a -7 or -8...close to killing myself...and I'm a +3 now...my feelings have gone from a -5 or -6 to a +5 or +6...I'm better because I did things...because I was honest...being real...I think I've gotten about 10% of what I could get...if I were to get 100%, it would be at least 9 to 10 times better...I can't imagine that...being real today is easier than what I was doing when I started...if I've only gotten 1-2% of what there is to get...that's crazy!...I couldn't think of 100%... I couldn't imagine 50-100 times what I have...I didn't even know there were people like that...it has gotten easier over time...I realize it is real...I am going to be a traveler not an observer...."

...another Pilgrim...

"...I think I have lived trying to believe that true happiness would be having a wonderful relationship with someone else...other than myself...I've always thought about that...I know if I fed others when I was hungry, I'd die... physically... and I've been doing that emotionally...I was dying inside and often not even aware of it...yes, since I've journaled every day for the last 10 days, I've learned things...I've shared about 4% of my truth, am now at a +5 up from a -10 at the begin-

ning...I know that I'm the only person that stands in the way of me being all that I can be and having all that life has to offer...it feels good...."

...another Pilgrim...

"I think I can imagine having it all...but that big?...it's like I am walking through another door...it's scary...everything is a distraction for me...I do know one thing...that I'm more in tune with myself than I've ever been before...but sometimes I still seem like a baby...I've moved from a -9 to a +4...that's a +14 gain...that's a 40-50% self awareness improvement...if I increased my self awareness to 100%, I'd be over 30...about 2 times the +14...if my overall self-awareness is only now about 10-15%...then the potential is maybe over +130...I'm climbing Mt. McKinley...that's not very far away...!"

Chapter Twelve

Opportunities
for Pilgrims
as Teachers

Solicitations of
Your Stories
of Discovery

"What is important for everyone to
know is that holy men and medicine
men must be measured by more than curing
abilities. They must also be
measured by their manner of life."

- Fools Crow by Thomas E. Mails

In the final or senior levels of personal growth and understanding, few opportunities in the experience and opinion of
this traveler offer the higher level student as much of an
opportunity of self-discovery and learning as that of teacher.
You will find that almost as soon as you begin to use your
newly acquired skills and awareness, even early in the doubt
phases, you will find yourself spontaneously sharing with
others the insights that are emerging. In some cases, some of
your earliest indications that what you are doing is actually
paying off may come to you through your catching yourself
unconsciously noting and intervening with someone whom
you find is struggling with a very early level conflict or distress. Say, for example, someone who is simply confusing
their experience with another person's or allowing another's

*

What if?

knowing

yourself

is finally,

enough

*

opinion to determine their experience. Before you know it, you hear yourself clarifying or attempting to clarify the problem for that person—even before you have become aware that **you** have consciously accepted this new principle as your own.

Therefore, along the way, we must listen to what we feel, think, and yes, even say to others because our minds are integrating information at a much higher rate than our simple awareness may be able to keep up with. It is truly an amazing thing to "wake up" in the middle of a conversation with a friend and find yourself attempting to instruct her on one of the basic elements of the self-awareness process that you—ten minutes earlier—may have listed as still residing in the "under trial consideration" column in your own mind. **The human mind is a wondrous and incredible creation, but the human spirit is many steps beyond in its complexity and capacity to function.** Reference, for example, the principle that for most, if not all, travelers, repressed or denied elements of the mind do not disappear or become irrelevant despite intense, long-standing and persistent efforts at denial. Avoided feelings actively impact an individual's sense of worth, self-respect, and self-esteem whether the individual acknowledges or is aware of it or not. Previous deceptions and dishonest behaviors are supposedly buried beneath years of denial and repression for many, and if you ask them, they will make responses which suggest there literally is no active record or impact of these events in their current experience. It is this traveler's experience, however, that with few to no exceptions, as these people are motivated (usually by outside influences) to find a reason to look at themselves more closely, they discover they **are** depressed and **are not** "in touch" with it. They do NOT respect themselves and are either not aware of it, or are not willing to acknowledge it. They have been successfully lying to **themselves** and unsuccessfully lying to others about the absence of the inevitable impact which their avoiding and dishonest behavior has had on them. On many occasions, the individual is the only person in his world who is actually "buying" his denial and deception. The question then becomes, "Who's fooling whom?"

The learning is complex, predictable and overwhelmingly rewarding. Those students that have gone before you have furthered their knowledge and mastery by sharing, almost always enthusiastically, not only in anticipation of their own growth, but, from the joy of what they share and the sharing in and of itself! Join the ranks of those who introduce others to what they have discovered about themselves and their brothers and sisters in our human family.

● ● ●

I would be pleased to know your personal stories of discovery and insight as you recount those moments that come so preciously unforeseen and unsolicited from within your own depths as you realize just how much there is to your overall experience and what you've been missing. As you have listened to the remarks and tales of those who shared with you, you have benefitted from enhanced attention and commitment at times of doubt, weakness, or tremendous pain. I invite you to share your experiences so that others may also benefit and further develop the growing body of the human spirit and its care and feeding. With gratitude in advance from those who will benefit from your sharing, your stories may be submitted in any legible format in any language (preferably English) to either of the Internet addresses or surface address below:

Internet Address:
   http://members.aol.com/GaNewMoon/index.html
   http://members.aol.com/DRJIMPAT/index.html

Surface Address:
   An Uncertain Pilgrim
   c/o My Therapist's Bookstore
   903 Main Street
   Stone Mountain, GA 30083
   Phone: 770-879-5300
   Fax: 770-879-8878

At the time of this writing, various support systems are in the developmental stage, including workshops, guided tours (video and audio presentations) for different levels of students, and leadership internships in allowing interested students to further develop their self-awareness as a personal reference and as a resource to others. If you will send to the above surface address your contact information and what future offerings you may be interested in, the resource center will be pleased to add you to its mailing list, as well as keep you updated on developments as they occur.

CHAPTER THIRTEEN

The Continuation
of Your Learning

The Journey

It doesn't happen all at once....You become. It takes a long time.

– Margery Williams

Listen as those who have gone before you describe their journeys:

"...I haven't been journaling...it was hard to do...hard to make myself...I tried...it was a bit like riding in the back seat of a fighter airplane...and not having control...putting a pen to paper...there was a hesitation...I want to be normal as long as it isn't uncomfortable... I think I was not putting all of my feelings down...but when I did write about the things I didn't want to get into, I guess I let myself experience some of those feelings...the negative ones...I guess I did embrace the feelings I've avoided...I didn't "make" it happen...it just happened...it really was easy, substantive and very real...I didn't question whether it was real...I knew it was real...I wouldn't have asked myself certain questions...logic is my favorite subject...like geometry in high school...those proofs...going line by line and coming up with the conclusion at the end...it was lots of fun to go line by line...at times, I don't journal...I forget

how to go about it...how to begin...it's like I have amnesia...a memory loss for what happens...it is like being in a hole...so, the journal is the calisthenics for the process!...when I do it...I feel more complete...I feel more of life...it is a kind of sacred or holy place...then, I'm more in touch with me..."

...another Pilgrim...

"I'm learning to accept when I get off focus...that I don't have to stay stuck in it...I can learn from it and move on...by thinking about what happens, how I felt...where I got off focus and wasn't true to myself...what worked and what didn't...I know my truth is that I'm lonely...I'm journaling...I let some things get between me and the journal...sometimes sleep...I guess I'm still part princess...like, I'll be faithful to myself when I feel like it...that doesn't work very well. I'm actually a lot better in these last 2 weeks...not having the lonely...the relationship "want" feelings...I'm feeling pretty independent... pretty satisfied being with just myself...I'm asking myself...how many times have I done this...gotten off track...back to focus...lose track and then back again...they say the definition of insanity is when you do the same things over and over and expect different outcomes...I feel good about what I'm doing...I still worry about what my Mother thinks about what I tell her I think...it really doesn't work very well to focus on others...not at all...but I find I still try at times...I still have a lot of fear...don't trust the relationship with my Mother completely... well, I guess it's me that I don't completely trust...I'm afraid it's too good to

be true...afraid I'll get complacent...I need to keep on doing what I'm doing...I don't want to lose "what" I'm "going"...I've thought about the question of what I'd be willing to lose myself over...what is worth losing myself over...absolutely nothing or nobody...without me, I have nothing...I had nothing when I first began and I know more about nothing now than I knew then...it is easier to know about what nothing is after one has something...my sister doesn't even yet know she's miserable...she's still trying to convince herself that she is O.K...when I look at what my thinking was like at first...I thought I knew everything...all these times I thought I had it down...I'm learning new things...well, old things...over and over...again...I will know everything there is to be a person when I suck in the last breath of life in me...it's hard to think of being a human...all these people...life is enormous...to think of who I am, of me...and what I've learned...it amazes me...because I think of how big everything is and how it's all changed...I think about whether it's me that's changed...by changing me, I've changed the whole world...yes, the whole world is me...to me. I think without life to perceive it, there is no world...if I can't perceive the world then there is no world...with me (for me) there is nothing...my truth is life... life is honesty, truth, safety and me...my awareness of it all...my feelings and thoughts...I'm thinking of having nothing vs something and how being able to say yes...I have self-worth and without me there is nothing for me...I'm a worthwhile human being...to me...I think I might have always been worthwhile to someone...before, that was all that really mattered..."

...another Pilgrim...

"I didn't have me when I first began...I've looked every-where for what I've needed except where it is...where I found it...now I know the difference between "doing" and "as if"...when my sister visited last week, we talked...about "nothing"...she's focusing on everyone else but herself...as I think of what I'm doing for me and about where my sister is...I'm sad...I feel grateful... I could have been where she is...but I don't know if I could have lived as long as she has...I don't know if I could have made it to 30 or not...I don't want to stop...life is getting simpler...I want to do this...all of these opportunities...I feel inspired, good...I have pur-pose...direction...and choices...I feel like I have myself...they are one and the same...I'm enjoying living life...being myself too...I guess, they are also one and the same...I'm journaling every night...for the last month or so...the inspiration began about two weeks ago...it's clear that after the focus, came me...then the energy...and the inspiration...the creativity... where there is focus, there is life...and understanding...I com-pletely attribute my inspiration...it's indescribable...so many feelings...to me...it's like someone opened up every pore in my body to let in new air and experi-ence...it's amazing...I've gotten back a lot of self-confi-dence and self-trust...I don't doubt me when someone else doubts me...before, I felt like I was dangling on a thin thread...before, I'd pray to God because I didn't trust myself...when I write, talk, experience what-ever...myself gets stronger...on the way back from vaca-tion...I drove a lot...and was very aware of the focus

issue...I thought...it's the focus thing...yes, there is a difference between being aware of one's self at all times and not...very few people know that...now is the time for me to think about what I need to do to stay focused and what things assist me in staying and getting focused...I know the distractions will come and working on the things that work for me are easier when I'm actually focused...it's harder to think about when you are distracted...when I was off focus, I journaled...dug into my feelings...let them be and accepted them...me...regardless...one thing I've kept with me...the knowledge I keep with me...no matter what I'm feeling...at least I'm feeling...it's not always fun...I talked to people about how I was feeling...there are lots of distractions...I know what to do...I'm just stubborn about really doing what I need...I still tell myself I'll do it their way—more—"next" time and try to keep some of the old way...it's only complete surrender that works...to "Mother Nature"...me...my feelings...all of them...it doesn't work unless you do it...if you let your truth be...you grow and you learn...you aren't empty anymore...before, I thought I knew it all...now, I just get out and learn more...it is 'to be or not to be'...I need to maintain my awareness of what my distraction signals are...if I kept a vigil...for me and for distraction...and immediately employed all of my tools I wouldn't get off track...maybe ever...when I no longer need all my energy to survive like at first...there is so much more energy for other things...I'm more creative..."

• • •

Now that you are aware and proceeding along your path, you will note many new experiences and modifications of old experiences that render themselves as new. Previously inviting and impassioned arenas of interest have already silently fallen away, and you note them almost without concern or sadness. You are aware that the elements of significance arise from within you and that these elements are simple, beautiful and graciously creative, full of joy and contentment. There is progressively less fear of loss of this new way of living as you continue to develop your new skills and awareness. You are in essence self-contained, and you proceed with the exploration of all that you are and all that time will allow you to become.

Relationships with others in any form are experienced much the same as a saunter through a fine museum. You heed and respond to those that offer the opportunity to express **your** self and experience **your** fullness to completion. You find that even the capacity to decline opportunities which do not meet your basic requirements are managed quietly and with respect without regret or guilt. Compassion for those that do not yet understand is an ever-present companion, and you willingly share the depth of your understanding with any that express genuine interest in ways that even strike you as full of wonder and grandeur.

It seems that Life has blossomed for you and any who are in your presence. The understanding is infectious and inviting in a way that stirs even the most ardent of critics! Those that seek to denigrate "their" experience of what you speak and who you are, do so with an air of doubt and uncertainty despite their at times vehement opposition. You are not surprised to see previously intense opponents coming quietly to you to seek your counsel in their search for meaning and solidarity. As they learn from you they become quietly aware with you that these lessons belong to everyone. They are as elements of our earth, our tribal rights, and not unlike the air, they are available and necessary to all for life itself. You now respond with respect, gratitude and patience where before, there may have been resentment, jealously or vindictiveness. Your manner is replete with the love and joy in living your experience each moment. When for brief moments you may find yourself distracted and returning to the "old" way, you explore the experience almost as an old man or woman returning to the place of their childhood—in a bit of disbelief—and you ponder how it was possible for you to endure before without full knowledge of what you now know and are. Your empathy and interest in those that continue to resist or struggle with life that is absent of TRUTH is constant and reverently vigilant. You have become, without seeking, a disciple of the essence of Life itself—that of TRUTH and LOVE.

Your journey is an ongoing, ever present reality. Your life is a gift from Creator to be cherished and honored in all of its splendor. The course and nature of your life has become ever so simple, and the choices you make are profoundly united in their purpose and direction. Let us share these gifts as we journey together, for the death of uncertainty is upon us.

EXERCISES

Taking the Journey

If you can just observe what you are and move with it, then you will find that it is possible to go infinitely far.

~ J. Krishnamurti

Equipment

You are ready to begin your journey. You are well guided and as you prepare to go where you have never traversed before, you will want to prepare yourself. Check the following list for equipment to take on this challenging pilgrimage! Gather together as many of the following items as you can and pack your camel! May your exploration be daring and rewarding!

My Backpack

TIMER

Locate a stove top wind-up timer in the color of your choice.

JOURNAL

Purchase a loose-leaf binder. This is suggested so that you may make easy page insertions if you choose. Others of you may prefer to purchase journals which appeal to you because of design or color. Please feel free to select the journal that speaks to you! Remember! It is essential to maintain COMPLETE PRIVACY and exclusive access to your journal. Some of us have chosen to use computers with password protection. Although using a computer to journal is acceptable, the actual art of writing is an important experience in the journaling, not only as you journal, but also as you return to your journal to re-experience your feelings and thoughts.

MEDICAL ALERT BRACELET

You may create your own or purchase a bracelet which may be engraved to read: "WHAT IS MY TRUTH?" You will wear this along your quest as you search for the answers.

SMALL MIRROR NECKLACE or
FAVORITE PICTURE OF YOU

This will serve as an ever present reminder of your source and will prompt you to focus over and over again.

PERSONAL SPACE

It is most important that you create a place of privacy... a kind of sacred space for yourself. A place free of distraction by others is ideal. The more natural the environment, the less stimulated you will be by external forces. This personal retreat will offer you a spot for quiet reflection. You will want to rest, reflect, and write in your journal in this space as often as possible.

CALENDAR RECORD

Purchase a conveniently accessible calendar upon which you may keep an easily-referenced record of which days of the week/month/year you are able to meet the "5 & 5" expectation. This precise record will give you even more information about the progress of your journey as you record the number of minutes spent reflecting and recording. For example, you may wish to format each entry with the day, date and time, as well as the number of minutes spent reflecting and recording (Sunday, May 4, 1997, 5:00 p.m. - 15 minutes & 15 minutes.) You will later examine these notations so you may begin to notice the ebb and flow in the pattern of your journey.

OPTIONAL

Some pilgrims use a small tape recorder or pocket notebook to record in-the-moment feelings and thoughts as they travel through each day. You may allow yourself whatever other equipment you choose to assist you in maintaining your self awareness and self focus.

Exercises

You may complete the exercises in your journal in sequence or you may set up a separate section labeled "Exercises." This is entirely up to you. With each of the following experiences remember the basics: Do not rush or hurry; allow the exercise to unfold; consider the questions posed OVER TIME; and BE HONEST. You will eventually find that the more deliberate, thorough, patient, and persevering you are with the tasks, the greater the quality of your experience. Some exercises will take a minimum of an hour or so. Others may be recommended to transpire over days, weeks and even months. At times, you will want to travel, then rest, then travel again through the exercise. This is the awakening. This is the journey. You are ready to begin.

Exercise One

Journaling

Chapter 2

Learning to Journal
The Process of Reflection & Recording

You may want to begin your journey today with a re-read of Chapter 2. The purpose is to familiarize the Pilgrim with the basic process of Journaling. You should begin this process as soon as possible because it is out of this exploration that the elements of this text will develop. It is literally through this daily reflection and recording that you will "get it"—the ideas and concepts presented in this guide.

Obtain a personal journal of your choosing. It may be in any style, color and/or format uniquely appealing to you. As mentioned, it is acceptable, though, for some not preferable, to use your word processor. Your guide considers the essential elements to be expandable page numbers (a loose-leaf binder), privacy (NO ONE should have access to the contents unless specifically permitted by you), ready availability (pocket size and/or portable), and affordability (spiral notebooks with 3-ring perforations and tear out sheets are perfectly acceptable.)

Begin the journaling process by finding a regularly accessible time. Most people find journaling at the same time each day beneficial. Many choose early morning or evening or just prior to retiring. It is recommended that you experiment with when **you** most benefit from the experience. Go to your designated private space which you consider to be free of distractions. Set your timer. First, spend a minimum of five minutes (not to exceed 15 minutes) in simple REFLECTION of how your day (last 24 hours) has been. During this period your purpose is to ask yourself the following question: **"What were significant, striking feelings and thoughts I experienced today?"** It is not at all uncommon, once the process is initiated, to find memories of the past surface in connection with the current days' events and circumstances. Include these elements in the reflection. The GOLDEN RULE is never to exclude an idea or thought for any reason. If you find particular experiences are uniquely painful or difficult to allow yourself to have fully unencumbered or edited, simply make a mental note of the subject and register that this is a charged or highly conflicted or painful subject and proceed with the continuation of the reflection. You will learn later the significance of this particular aspect of the process and how to manage it.

Second, at the conclusion of the REFLECTION period, begin a 5-minute (again, not to exceed 15 minutes) timed RECORDING in the journal of ALL of the thoughts and feelings that have gone through your mind during the reflection period. Here is a time to make any notations of highly charged or conflicted feelings you previously had. Be sure that you always include both Past and Current feelings and thoughts.

The suggested format of the page is one that leaves a column of unused space as a wide margin (two inches are suggested) for ALL pages. This space will become very important in future phases. The numbering of pages is strongly encouraged. Never make an entry without a date or make marginal notes or reflections (at later stages) without dating each one.

The following is a graphic representation of the suggested format and is suitable for copying if you desire.

Sample Journal Page

What are/were my feelings and thoughts today/yesterday?

What Is My Truth

Date: _____

Reflection Time: _____ Recording Time: _____

_____

_____

Leave 2" margin   _____

blank for later   _____

additions, notations   _____

& observations   _____

_____

_____

_____

_____

_____

_____

_____

Be sure to include any thoughts and feelings about the journaling process itself. Many individuals begin their journal with entries specifically pertaining to this. Remember, the process quality and the benefit you derive depend upon practice, persistence and patience with honest self-appraisal, regardless of the subject or substance. This includes the journaling process if indeed the process stimulates significant thoughts and feelings along the way.

Exercise Two

My Earliest Awareness

Chapter 3

This opportunity is for you to recall your first moment of clarity and awareness. As you reflect upon your early life, you may discover that experiential memories are held within a multi-roomed museum in your mind. As you enter each room, you may have a single recollection which will yield previously forgotten treasures. These gifts are often overlooked keys to doors within your current awareness and appreciation of all of who you are and all of what you have experienced. Life, in its simplest form, is a discovery of experiences which begin with our earliest awareness. The benefits of taking a retrospective look are not in the dwelling upon the past, but in the uncovery of the present.

Write a journal entry which describes as fully as you may recall your first poignant memory and awareness.

Exercise Three

Initial Self Appraisal

Chapter 3

Positive and Negative Traits
as Seen By Self and Others

This exercise lends itself nicely as a journal entry. Your objective is to begin to get in touch with how you see yourself as well as how others see you. Set up four (4) columns. Label each in the following manner:

Positive Characteristics-Traits-Assets I see in Me
Negative Characteristics-Traits-Liabilities I see in Me
Positive Characteristics-Traits-Assets Others see in Me
Negative Characteristics-Traits-Liabilities Others see in Me

Begin to list descriptors (Assets AND Liabilities) that you and others would apply to you currently. It may be helpful for you to ask yourself, "What are the traits I have that are experienced by me and others?" You may not even agree with characteristics others have used to describe you. But, it is essential that you are honest about your analysis and that you include all desirable and undesirable terms. If you choose, you may rate them in terms of their intensity and/or prominence or presence within your overall personality and awareness. You may assign a negative (-) or a positive (+) number beside each descriptor if you find this enlightening and an even more honest method of self-appraisal.

It is perfectly acceptable to leave this list open as you may find yourself becoming aware of elements and/or traits that you have omitted. It is important to go back to this initial list and continue developing it. Don't forget to date each entry accordingly as the observation is added. You will find as your "personal strength" grows that you will be more in touch with your negative or undesirable traits. Remember, there is absolutely no place for omission. The quality of the outcome for you will be profoundly affected by the level of your personal honesty as you proceed. Think of this as a kind of personal physical examination. Would you want your physician to leave out certain body systems or aspects of your physical self for ANY reason? We who have gone before you understand that the answer is, of course, "NO." However, you will find at times very powerful urges to understate, minimize or even altogether avoid or eliminate painful or uncomfortable elements. NEVER EVER DO THIS. You will eventually be grateful for the courage of the completeness of your personal TRUTH, whatever that may be. So, you may now begin your self appraisal and have a GOOD LOOK!

Exercise four

Personal Change

Chapter 3

Reference Exercise 3 and Create a
Personal Change List

This activity is for those of you who believe that one has to have a goal to get somewhere. Complete this section now if you must. However, some Pilgrims report that postponement of this section is advantageous until one is more familiar with the experience of self-focus. Completing the activity at that time is more easily achieved and less of a distraction.

Make a list of all of those qualities and/or traits you have that you do not like and would prefer to "lose" or even give away. Be as complete as possible, once again, not omitting any negative or undesirable components. As in Exercise Three, you may rate these entries as you believe they reflect their magnitude and presence in your personality. This list is also an appropriate inclusion for your Journal and may be modified and added to over time as perceptions emerge.

Exercise Five

Prior Learning and Achievement List

Chapter 4

*What I Thought I'd Never Learn
To Do...But Did!!*

Begin by making a list of everything you've learned to do that at one time you were unable to do! Sounds like quite a list! And it very well may be. You may include items such as learning to ride a "two-wheeler" bike, learning to speak a foreign language and even to think in it, learning to play ANY musical instrument, discovering your ability as an athlete, or even developing talents far beyond what you expected you ever would.

The significance of these learning experiences will become more apparent as you proceed within the recommended course of self-awareness.

Exercise Six

Self Awareness Pursuits

Chapter 4

What I Like and Dislike and Why

This exercise has two parts. First, make four lists with the following headings:

Activities   Experiences   Places   People

Then, list the words/items/members that fall under each category which describe what you like or find as a source of pleasure, and why. For example, under *People* you might write: *"My daughter—because she has courage."* Under *Activities* you might list: *"Swimming—because I can just float."* The objective is to list as many words, items, and members as need be included on the lists. Keep the lists open for additions (and subtractions) as they may occur in your expanded awareness.

Next, list the words, etc. that fall under each of these same four categories which describe what you do NOT like or may find as a source of displeasure. For example, under *Experiences* you may mention: "My first day of school—because I was terrified." Or, under *Places* you might add: "My grandmother's basement—because it is dark and damp."

This particular method of enhancing self awareness provides exercise in seeking access to the self which you might otherwise overlook or avoid. Again, as always, it is imperative that you be TOTALLY HONEST and not "leave off" or "add to" the list because you "should."

Exercise Seven

Personal Attachment List

Chapter 5

My Pie of Life
What I Value and How Much I Value It

You might consider NOT reading Chapter 5 prior to completing this exercise. You may find it distracting to YOUR Truth at this stage in your journey. It is however, appropriate and certainly, recommended, that you read the chapter following your completion of the Pie Graph.

Make a list of all of the emotionally significant aspects or elements of your life. As you list each area, assign a percentage value to represent its overall importance to you personally. For example, My Health - 30%, My Intelligence - 30%, My Family - 15%, My Friends - 10%, My Income - 5%, and My Home/Personal Belongings - 10%. Total: 100%. These categories are simply EXAMPLES and are not necessarily the selection criteria for you to use.

Exercise Eight

Personal Change
Loss Inventory and Responses

Chapter 6

What I've Lost and How It's Impacted Me

Some Pilgrims experience this exercise as more difficult to attend to and complete. It can often be painful and is most likely an area of your awareness you consciously have chosen to avoid. It will take courage and a willingness to dredge up some feelings long since buried. As you explore your increased awareness regarding the losses in your life, you will begin to understand the depth and the character of attachment and its impact on you.

Make a list of what you consider to be the significant experiential losses in your life to date. The list may include people, financial assets, property, pets, jobs, etc. As you have sustained these losses, you have experienced feelings, thoughts, and symptoms with each one. Please indicate next to the loss those emotional responses as well as the time you experienced as necessary to negotiate or "deal with" the loss. An entry example might be:

"My best friend's death when I was 16: anxiety, anger, fear, despair, social withdrawal & isolation, and impaired concentration: lasted 6 - 24 months."

Another might be: "My child's injury resulting in my having to quit my job: fear, helplessness, anger, resentment, hopelessness, frustration, alone: continues to be ongoing."

Exercise Nine

Personal Dishonest List

Chapter 8

What is My Truth? Do I Know?
Does Anyone Else?

Another essential activity to perform is the Dishonest List. This is a tough assignment for even the most diligent of Pilgrims. It requires a willingness to KNOW YOUR TRUTH and OWN it in a way you may NEVER have before.

Please begin by making an HONEST LIST of those experiences, activities, events, and relationships in which you are aware of having been dishonest. Your dishonesty may have been intentional or unintentional, partial or complete. You may have "only" been dishonest with yourself, or you may have been dishonest with others. It is particularly important that you identify "to whom" (person(s) including yourself) the dishonesty was directed toward.

Examples may include extramarital affairs, driving under the influence (whether caught or not), use of illicit substances, participation in unprotected sexual relationships, stealing anything, anytime, extending only minimal effort rather than full ability, cheating in any arena—to name only a few. This list is another record that is best kept open so that you may later make additions (SMILE.) We're Pilgrims, not Saints!

DO NOT allow the length or the extent of this list to be a factor in the comprehensive and thorough development of the list. Know that any limitation of the list is a limitation of the full discovery of your spirit. Here again, the critical element is "simple" honesty.

Exercise Ten

Personal Unsafe List

Chapter 8

What Have I Been Doing and How Safe Am I?

It is recommended that the Pilgrim include in the Journal a listing of all of those events, relationships, activities, and experiences, that you have ever participated in or contributed to that had, as a potential outcome, an injurious or deleterious result to anyone. Please indicate the frequency and the age or age ranges of the Pilgrim at or during the time(s) of the occurrences. Examples would be:

"Driving under the influence: weekly, irregularly, 6 times per year, ages 15-22."

"Participating in unprotected sexual activities, 2-3 times monthly, ages 13-27."

Take time to list all of your previous and current unsafe behaviors and, possibly, even your unsafe thoughts. As we begin to realize the consequences of our conscious and unconscious unsafe behaviors, we have another critical awareness opportunity which could be life-altering.

Exercise Eleven

Behavioral - Feeling Indicators with Ratings

Chapter 11

Have You Journeyed Three Months?
Are You Focused?
Subjective Qualitative Experiential Rating Scale
(SQERS)

It is recommended that you travel a minimum of 3 months prior to completing this exercise. You may continue on and return to this activity if you have not done so. Otherwise, please begin by referring to your Unsafe and Dishonest Lists prior to beginning this exercise. Note the issues you identified as problematic for you. Rate them NOW in terms of how you experience them when you are Focused and when you are Not.

Please proceed now to create entries of behaviors and feelings. Suggestions include: Mood, Self-esteem, Motivation, Self-respect, Energy, Depression, Anxiety, Intimacy, Perseverance, Achievement, Contentment, etc. You may add areas in your awareness which you consider to be clearly affected by your focus and lack of focus. With each category or entry it is suggested that you also include modifiers as appropriate concerning the quality or consistency of the feeling or behavior. You may choose to give a number rating on a -10 to +10 scale to establish a basis for examination and comparison. A -10 represents the lowest level possible, 0 represents a neutral value, and +10 represents the highest level that you can now consider reaching (i.e., contentment.) You may choose to give yourself a range, say, -2 to +2 when that seems to be a more accurate indicator of your overall experience. The following is an example of how to go about completing this exercise:

Mood—generally upbeat, changeable at times of significant stress: -3 to +2, average: -1.

You may want to refer to Figure 9, page 156 to set up your categories and begin this exercise.

Exercise Twelve

Personal Daily Schedule

Chapter 3

You will find that TIME is perhaps the only valuable real estate in the universe, and if it is not studied and understood, you will miss much of what life has to offer.

Make a list or schedule of how you spend a typical week—all 7 days from rising to rising. You may begin the schedule hour by hour or more broadly by simply listing activities in a typical day and estimating how much time you spend in each. Categories such as work, eating, sleeping, and driving should be included along with less typical activity such as snow skiing or bike riding. Include the categories of time spent on each activity.

Example: **Monday(s)**

Work - 8 hours
Cleaning house - 2 hours
Laundry - 3 hours
Etc.

Proceed through the week and then make a separate category to include infrequent activity.

Example: **Infrequent activities**

Snow skiing - 3 days per year
Traveling - 7 days per year
Reading for pleasure - 6 hours per month
Etc.

This tracking of time is appropriate for your Journal and will later become a reference for you as you make future discoveries and choices.

Exercise Thirteen

Personal Distractions List

Chapter 9

What's My Focus? Do I Ever Question It?

Include in the Journal a listing of all the people, relationships, activities, pastimes, events, and experiences that have at any time produced a distraction which caused, or was a associated with, your losing focus or awareness of your own feeling and thoughts. Examples would be romantic attractions, noise, intrusive or demanding relationships, substance use or abuse, theft, specific stresses, and past, current, and/or future fears or expectations.

These examples are offered to generate a few of the Focus points other than Self that we tend to spend much of our core attention on.

Exercise fourteen

Personal Growth Environments

Chapter 10

My Support System
Who? What? and Where?

You will find that some activities, places, or people are more conducive to self-reflection than others. As you proceed with your self-study, it will be helpful for you to specifically consider all of those places, people, and circumstances that you may have previously noticed support a kind of reverence and personal awareness. It will be important for you to surround yourself with these environments, and when you choose to be "with" others, select those, particularly initially, who respect your journey even if they are not on a similar one. As you become a well-seasoned traveler, this will not be as critical as it is in the beginnings of your journey.

Make a list of all of these places, people, and circumstances which you personally know to be supportive or conducive to self-reflection. Examples may include a local park, a unique and private room in your home, a favorite coffee house on a Sunday morning (alone or with a special non-intrusive friend/fellow Pilgrim), a church sanctuary open for private use, a local library or bookstore. Keep these places and circumstances in your awareness and seek them out as often as you can and as regularly as possible. The "best" option many have found is to include at least one of these opportunities in your daily schedule. You will certainly want to include them no less often than weekly.

Certain activities are uniquely well-suited for enhancing self-awareness. It is valuable to incorporate these experiences into your moment-to-moment living. Opportunities which may provide increased self-focus might be volunteering as a support worker a few hours a week in a social services agency (reading to children in a nursery or patients in a hospital), beginning or continuing your autobiography, or enrolling in a non-credit course to explore some subject you have always wanted to know more about. Take up a hobby you have always wanted to pursue even if you spend as little as one hour per week on it. Spend at least an hour per day purely devoted to you. Begin a daily, light exercise such as walking for 10 - 30 minutes or yoga. You will be amazed how simple, self-focused activities will add to your basic exploration of who you are. Your personal experience will be enhanced with these very simple additions to your life.

ADDENDUM

Availability of Support Resources

Buyer Beware

The acquisition of a working relationship with a well-trained, ethical, bright, sensitive, appropriately-credentialed professional can be an invaluable catalyst and resource through parts or all of your self-emergence. The benefits of having a seasoned Traveler alongside as you journey are numerous. Pilgrims who have gone before who continue their own quest and who have a deep understanding and respect for "the work" can provide guidance and facilitate insight. It is strongly recommended, however, that the student proceed with great caution in both the decision to acquire such support and the selection of the individual. Just as a Pilgrim who has self-focus, integrity, and skill maybe an asset to you, one who does not may be a distraction.

Professional resource organizations have admission and membership criteria that are approved by the group membership itself and, for obvious operational reasons, it is usually not possible to get relative qualitative information about individual members other than indirectly (that which is "implied" by membership itself.) There are, of course, additional "nonprofessional" resources. You should take great care in choosing any resource, professional or otherwise. It is NOT recommended to simply use a local telephone directory randomly or to use the professional directories without other information. Professional associations carefully watch the equal distribution of referrals among all members. It is therefore incumbent upon the consumer to obtain additional information about a particular individual.

How to go about this process is complex and varies with the particular specialty and/or organization. Considerations include personal recommendations from someone you know and trust who has had personal or professional contact with a candidate; knowledge by word-of-mouth or other

218 An Uncertain Pilgrim

sources concerning a particular candidate's area of special interest and ability; whether the candidate's name surfaces from more than one of multiple research resources and whether the professional in question is someone who would be used by his or her peers.

In the mental health field, this writer recommends three ultimate criteria after you do the initial screening. The first is that the proposed candidate should have completed some form of appropriate formal educational program and be willing to share this information readily. The second is whether the individual seeking the professional assistance or counsel experiences the candidate as able to "hear" and understand the individual seeking the assistance after a reasonable opportunity and exposure (usually after 3-6 substantive contacts.) Third, after a significant time (usually no more than 3-6 months) working with the candidate-therapist, the consumer should experience some element of discernible change and/or understanding occurring. An additional consideration is whether the candidate is "open" to the consumer seeking "second opinions" at any time during the process. Practitioners who rely heavily on medication in the absence of the ability to relate to the student and communicate effectively concerning personal growth and awareness are best avoided in favor of professionals who clearly have both capacities. The possible use of a physician (e.g., Psychiatrist or Family Physician) in combination with a non-physician therapist (e.g., Clinical Psychologist, Clinical Social Worker, or Licensed Professional Counselor) is also suggested as a consideration.

Remember, YOU are the consumer, the individual actually directing the process, and you are the BOSS. It is ultimately your decision. Use your instinctive talents, listen to your "gut" and proceed with caution, deliberation, and diligence.

In the pursuit of enhancement of his emotional and intellectual functioning, the student may consider completing a comprehensive physical and mental examination by a qualified health care professional to exclude as much as possible the possible presence or contributing influences of undetected or even known physical or mental illness.

Resources

PROFESSIONAL

Mental Health Professionals
Psychiatrists
Psychologists
Psychiatric Nurse Practitioners
Licensed Clinical Social Workers
Licensed Professional Counselors

Various Medical/Professional Associations and Specialty Groups
Local/State Medical Society
Internal Medicine
Family Practice
Psychiatry
Child Psychiatry
Local Mental Health Associations

Clerical Associations
General/collective Local Organization by Denomination

Churches

Public/Private Schools - Counselors, Teachers, and Special Education Providers

Your local Family Physician

Service Organizations

OTHER

Senior Family "WISE PERSON"

Family Member (exert great caution)

Your Memory Bank

Personal "Soul Search"

Internet - The Uncertain Pilgrim Home Page and Others

Anyone (carefully selected, same criteria as the professional)

Relevant Additional Factors

There are many relevant additional factors which are wise to consider in the complete approach to developing an individual's full potential. One must not assume that the origins of current distress, dysfunction or sub-optimal experience or achievement exist independent of any physical problem or illness. Although unlikely statistically, this must be considered in any thorough approach to enhancing an individual's overall function as a possible atypical expression of a common or physical problem or illness/disease. Likewise, it is understood that one can have significant physical and/or emotional dysfunction which fulfills traditional diagnostic medical criteria and which needs to be recognized and properly attended to in conjunction with the recommendations made herein to enhance an individual's daily emotional and experiential function and efficacy.

While there may be specific constraints placed upon the individual by virtue of the presence of one or more specific medical or emotional "illnesses" or "diagnostic" entities, it is a general assumption and the overall experience of this traveler that with few exceptions, save for progressive and/or end stage dementia, that even in the presence of such a coexisting impairment, the rules and processes offered herein will, if followed, continue to serve and enhance the student of human nature well. The presence of a coexisting illness or diagnosis does not mean that the individual's awareness of himself cannot be enhanced. It simply demands that the management requirements of the specific condition be met in addition to the self-awareness aspects of identity and self-respect. There may be, on occasion, some practitioners who may assert that certain elements of personal self-awareness herein recommended are contraindicated in the successful management of a particular condition; however, the student is directed to seek "second opinions" and use common sense when excluding a particular element contained in this reference. An example of this might be in the case of the individual who carries a diagnosis of say "Schizophrenia" or "Post Traumatic Stress Disorder (PTSD)" where the treating professional is recommending "supportive only" therapy directed to simply assist the individual in coping moment-to-moment with their stresses—both internally and externally in their origins. In this situation, the treating professional may indeed take a position that a more in-depth exploration of the patient's past and/or current experiences might be detrimental. The wise consumer would research the diversity of professional opinion available concerning whether a more complete understanding of one's self could be detrimental to the individual and, after weighing the essence of the opinions, make an informed decision.

There is an absolute need for a thorough complete physical and mental examination by a competent medical practitioner.

One should be aware that various physical and mental conditions can produce difficulty which can be perceived as simply emotional or developmental barriers. The recognition and appropriate clinical management of these medical conditions will enhance the individual's capacity to make use of the opportunities offered in this presentation. See also **Availability of Support Resources.**

Specifically, the judicious use of supportive clinical interventions, including appropriate psychoactive medications, can and does facilitate the individual student's capacity to manage her emotional state more successfully. This in turn creates more "energy" and time available to the student and thus a greater opportunity for her to benefit from introspective learning efforts.

Notes

Notes

Notes